Frederick James Furnivall

Education in Early England

Frederick James Furnivall

Education in Early England

ISBN/EAN: 9783337219048

Printed in Europe, USA, Canada, Australia, Japan

Cover: Foto ©Suzi / pixelio.de

More available books at **www.hansebooks.com**

Education

in

Early England.

SOME NOTES USED AS FOREWORDS TO A COLLECTION
OF TREATISES ON "MANNERS & MEALS IN OLDEN TIME"
FOR THE EARLY ENGLISH TEXT SOCIETY,

BY

FREDERICK J. FURNIVALL, M.A.

TRIN. HALL, CAMBRIDGE; MEMBER OF COUNCIL OF THE PHILOLOGICAL
AND EARLY ENGLISH TEXT SOCIETIES.

LONDON :

N. TRÜBNER & CO., 60, PATERNOSTER ROW.

1867.

Price One Shilling.

[As the subject of these notes may interest many people into whose hands the volume of which the notes constitute the Preface may not fall, 500 copies have been pulled for separate circulation. But it is the plain duty of all Schoolmasters and Educators to join the Early English Text Society at once.]

JOHN CHILDS AND SON, PRINTERS.

3, *Old Square, Lincoln's Inn, W.C.*
10 *June,* 1867.

DEAR SIR,

THE state of the Early English Text Society's work, and its subscriptions for the present year, is this :—
There is now at press £950 worth of work, and about £300 worth more ought to go to press—will be ready for it, and is wanted by students—before the close of the year.

The Society's income to meet this expenditure will not be more than £500. The balance, and the Texts represented by it, will have to be carried over to, and kept back till, next year, unless some measure of relief can be adopted.

The Committee have unanimously rejected the proposal to double Members' subscription, because they know that many Members have resolved to limit their expenditure on Texts to a yearly guinea, and any quasi-compulsory effort to raise the subscription would be alike repulsive to the feelings of the Committee and the unwilling Members.

But the Committee see no objection to a voluntary effort to relieve the present income of part of the burden laid on it, and they have sanctioned my submitting to you the plan herein-after laid down. By your leave, I will put it to you in the personal way in which it came to me.

Mr Richard Morris was the cause of it, as he was of the founding of the Society. When in 1863 he was sending extracts from English MSS. abroad to be printed in a foreign journal, because there was no journal or Society in England to print them, it *did* seem to me a shame, and that if people only knew it, they'd stop it. The result was the getting-up of the Early English Text Society, which, to say the least of it, has done some worthy work for our Language and Literature.

Now in 1867 comes a block-up. Mr Morris and Mr Skeat, for instance,—not to name other Editors,—are willing to give us more work [1] than we can print, and it does seem a shame that they should be kept standing still for want of money only. The question for the rest of us is : Are we, after having had from these Editors such magnificent voluntaries as *The Ayenbite* and the Vernon *Langlande's Piers*

---

[1] "I think you ought in all justice to add a note somewhere, that the *quantity* of work done by some editors is not owing to any haste on their part, but to the vast amount of time which they give to the Society." My own belief is that all readers of our books know that the average of our work is up to, if not above, that of the average of any other Society.

Ploughman,[1] to keep them waiting three years for organ-blowers, when they are willing and ready to give us at once fresh music from our far-off early land ? " Not if we can help it," say several Members to whom I have spoken. The chances of life and fortune are so many, that brain-work offered should be accepted while it can be had. It is want of Editors, not of money, that has shut up Societies hitherto ; and the quicker the Early English Text Society can get its work in hand, and out, the better.

My proposal therefore is, to have an EXTRA SERIES, to take principally, and in the first instance, the *Re-editions* on the Society's list—thus leaving the Original Series free for first work at the Manuscript only ;[2]—the subscription to be one guinea due on every 1st of June. To make sure of some measure of relief to the parent-funds by this means, I have put to the credit of this Extra-Series Fund *fifty guineas* from the anticipated profits on the Percy Folio, and as soon as £200 more is realized from that source, I will add that sum to the fund, provided that Caxton's print of Maleore's *Morte D'Arthur* be re-edited in the Extra Series. We have had enough adulterated or modernized editions of this book to make us want a genuine one ; Southey's, at from 4 to 6 guineas, is not accessible to many of us; moreover, it does not in certain particulars properly represent the original ; and looking at the work before the Society, they could not take up this book, in the ordinary course, under 10 years from this time.

As further aids to the Extra-Series Fund, will be issued Large-Paper Quarto copies of all the books, on choice ribbed paper, the subscription for which will be two guineas a year. Several demands have been made for such copies of all our E. E. T. Soc. Texts ; and the beginning of a new series will enable it to start with Large-Papers.[3] As also these re-editions will be works with a reputation more or less established, they will sell to the public, and thus bring in a further revenue in aid of the fund. (I say these things in order to show subscribers that they'll get their guinea's worth for their guinea, though the number of subscribers to the Extra Series will not equal that to the Original one.)

The first works that I propose for the Extra Series are—
CHAUCER'S PROSE WORKS, to be edited from the best MSS., with a Preface on the Grammar and Dialect of Chaucer, and Notes, by Richard Morris, Esq.—the Rev. W. W. Skeat assisting in the

[1] Just ready.
[2] This is to meet the objection that the Texts of the Original and Extra Series would cross and clash with one another. I don't believe it possible, as the management of both Series is in the same hands, and should have preferred making the Extra Series simply a relief one to the Original Series for *any* Texts.
[3] If you would like a Three-Guinea Large-Paper issue of the E. E. Text Soc.'s future texts of the Original Series, and are willing to pay Three Guineas a year for it (we publish so much that One Guinea over the ordinary subscription would not cover the extra cost of paper and print), will you let Mr Wheatley or me know ? If 50 Members will subscribe for such an issue, I have little doubt that the Committee will order it. And of the Texts for 1864, -5, & -6, to be reprinted, Large-Papers may also be printed, if people like to subscribe for them.

Treatise on the Astrolabe,—and an Essay on the Pronunciation of Chaucer and Shakspere by Alexander J. Ellis, Esq., F.R.S.

WILLIAM AND THE WEREWOLF, to be re-edited from the unique MS. in King's College, Cambridge, by the Rev. W. W. Skeat, M.A.

MORTE D'ARTHUR, "ended the .ix. yere of the reygne of kyng Edward the Fourth [A.D. 1468] by syr Thomas Maleore, knyght," and by Caxton "deuyded in to xxi bookes, chaptyred and emprynted and fynysshed in thabbey Westmestre the last day of July the yere of our lord MCCCCLXXXV," to be re-edited from the original edition, with an Index, Glossary, and new Preface.

Of Chaucer's Prose Works no separate edition has ever been published (so far as I know), and yet his *Astrolabe* contains words that bring him home to us perhaps more than any other, the expression of his fatherly love for his boy. For these Works there must be a demand outside of the Society. *William and the Werewolf* has long been out of the market, and never has been accessible to the general student. The reason that *Havelok the Dane* is not proposed for reprinting is that Sir Frederic Madden, when generously putting the result of his editorial labours at the Society's service, expressly desired that the new edition of Havelok should be left to him to publish in his own way and at his own time. And, much as the book is wanted by students, much as the Committee have desired to see it in print, much as the cause of Early English suffers from the continued keeping-back of the book, the Committee have felt bound to respect the original Editor's wish. Otherwise the text would have been out in 1865.

I have received the following names of Subscribers to the Extra Series, and ask you if you will add yours to them. Will you help to blow the organ? Names and Subscriptions should be sent to Hy B. Wheatley, Esq., 53, Berners St, or to Messrs Trübner; or names may come to me.

For 8vo Copies.

Adams, G. E., Esq.
Addis, E., Esq.
Atkinson, Rev. J. C.
Bain, J., Esq.
Bain, —, Esq.
Baker, C., Esq.
Christ's College Library.
Davies, Robert, Esq.
Ellis, Alexander J., Esq.
Evans, Sebastian, Esq.
Falconer, Thos., Esq.
Forster, John, Esq.
Gee, W., Esq.
Guild, J. Wyllie, Esq.
Harris, Wm., Esq.
Hodgson, S. H., Esq.
Jackson, S., Esq.

Lumby, Rev. J. R.
Macmillans, Messrs., Cambridge, 2 *copies.*
Melbourne Public Library.
Parker, H. T., Esq., 11 *copies.*
Percy MS. Fund, 50 *copies.*
Rossetti, W. M., Esq.
Simms, C. S., Esq.
Timmins, S., Esq.
Trübner, Messrs., 25 *copies.*
Vernon, G. V., Esq.
Watson, R. S., Esq.
Weymouth, R. F., Esq.
Whalley, J. E., Esq.
Whitaker, J., Esq.
White, G. H., Esq.
Williamson, Rev. W.

For Large-paper copies.

Adam, John, Esq.	Paine, Cornelius, Esq.
Backhouse, J. H., Esq.	Panton, Rev. G. A.
Bain, J., Esq.	Parker, Hy. T., Esq.
Cosens, F. W., Esq.	Redfern, Rev. R. S.
Gibbs, Henry H., Esq.	Taylor, Thos. F., Esq.
Leigh, John, Esq.	Trübner, N., Esq.
Macmillans, Messrs., Cambridge.	

Subscribers may rely on the same care and energy being given to the Extra Series as have been devoted to the Original one. Nonmembers may subscribe to the Extra Series only. The Texts will be on sale at fixed prices separately, as the Society's other Texts regularly are.

Hoping that I may look on the work—this Extra Series—as, through your help, begun, and as sure to be carried through, (it is indeed the only way *through* the Society's heavy work,) there remains only to consider the objections to doing it. Objection-making is easy work ; and 'how *not* do it' is much less trouble than 'how *to* do it.' It has been urged, then,

1. 'That we are overdoing it.' This is a shadow from 'þe Clowde of Vnknowyng' (MS. to be printed in 1869). We have a field of 50 acres to reap in a harvest-time, how short, who can tell? Let us get one acre done as soon as we can.

2. 'That it is not fair to original subscribers.' One of them answered this in nearly these words :—'Though I don't mean to subscribe myself, I'm not such a dog in the manger as to want to keep other Members and the public out of the new Texts for perhaps 10 years, till the original fund could give them, just to suit myself, especially when I can buy separately such Texts as I want.'

3. 'Men won't subscribe ; they don't care enough for old work ; their book-shelves are full, &c., &c.' Some won't, of course,—what has antiquity done for them?—even some who *do* care for the old men won't feel justified in subscribing ; but others will, others *will* back men now giving their brains and time to increase our old men's fame, and let us know more of the thoughts they thought and the words they spoke. I hope you are one of these, and that you will help us if you can.

Yours truly,

F. J. FURNIVALL.

** I should be glad of more names at once for the Preliminary List of Subscribers. *William and the Werewolf* will go to press forthwith. *Chaucer's Prose Works* are being copied.

FOREWORDS.

"The naturall maister Aristotell saith that euery body be the course of nature is enclyned to here & so all that refressheth & quickeneth the spretys of man[1] / wherfor I haue thus in this boke folowinge[2]" gathered together divers treatises touching the Manners & Meals of Englishmen in former days, & have added therto divers figures of men of old, at meat & in bed,[3] to the end that, to my fellows here & to come, the home life of their forefathers may be somewhat more plain, & their own minds somewhat rejoiced.

The treatises here collected consist of two main ones—John Russell's *Boke of Nurture* and Hugh Rhodes's *Boke of Nurture*, to which I have written separate prefaces[4]—and certain shorter poems addressed partly to those whom Cotgrave calls "*Enfans de famille*, Yonkers of account, youthes of good houses, children of rich parents

---

[1] The first sentence of Aristotle's *Metaphysics* is 'All men by nature are actuated by the desire of knowledge.' Mr Skeat's note on l. 78 of *Partenay*, p. 228.

[2] Lawrens Andrewe. *The noble lyfe & natures of man, of bestes*, &c. Johñes Desborrowe. Andewarpe.

[3] The woodcuts are Messrs Virtue's, and have been used in Mr Thomas Wright's *History of Domestic Manners and Customs*, &c.

[4] If any one thinks it a bore to read these Prefaces, I can assure him it was a much greater bore to have to hunt up the material for them, and set aside other pressing business for it. But the Boke of Curtasye binding on editors does not allow them to present to their readers a text with no coat and trowsers on. If any Members should take offence at any expressions in this or any future Preface of mine, as a few did at some words in the last I wrote, I ask such Members to consider the first maxim in their Boke of Curtasye, *Don't look a gift horse in the mouth.* Prefaces are gift horses; and if mine buck or shy now and then, I ask their riders to sit steady, and take it easy. On the present one at least they'll be carried across some fresh country worth seeing.

(yet aliue)," partly to merchants' sons and good wives' daughters, partly to schoolboys, partly to people in general, or at least those of them who were willing to take advice as to how they should mend their manners and live a healthy life.

The persons to whom the first poems of the present collection are addressed, the

> yonge Babees, whome bloode Royalle
> Withe grace, feture, and hyhe habylite
> Hathe enourmyd,

the "Bele Babees" and "swete Children," may be likened to the "young gentylmen, Henxmen,—VI Enfauntes, or more, as it shall please the Kinge,"—at Edward the Fourth's Court; and the authors or translators of the Bokes in this volume, somewhat to that sovereign's Maistyr of Henxmen, whose duty it was

" to shew the schooles[1] of urbanitie and nourture of Englond, to lerne them to ryde clenely and surely ; to drawe them also to justes ; to lerne them were theyre harneys ; to haue all curtesy in wordes, dedes, and degrees ; dilygently to kepe them in rules of goynges and sittinges, after they be of honour.   Moreover to teche them sondry languages, and othyr lerninges vertuous, to harping, to pype, sing, daunce, and with other honest and temperate behaviour and patience ; and to kepe dayly and wekely with these children dew convenity, with corrections in theyre chambres, according to suche gentylmen ; and eche of them to be used to that thinge of vertue that he shall be moste apt to lerne, with remembraunce dayly of Goddes servyce accustumed.   This maistyr sittith in the halle, next unto these Henxmen, at the same boarde, to have his respecte unto theyre demeanynges, howe manerly they ete and drinke, and to theyre communication and other formes curiall, after *the booke of urbanitie.*"   (Liber Niger in *Household Ordinances*, p. 45.)

That these young Henxmen were gentlemen, is expressly stated,[2]

[1] scholars?
[2] Sir H. Nicolas, in his Glossary to his *Privy Purse Expenses of Henry VIII.*, p. 327, col. 2, says, "No word has been more commented upon than ' Henchmen ' or Henxmen.   Without entering into the controversy, it may be sufficient to state, that in the reign of Henry the Eighth it meant the pages of honour.   They were the sons of gentlemen, and in public processions always walked near the monarch's horse : a correct idea may be formed of their appearance from the representation of them in one of the pictures in the meeting room of the Society of Antiquarians.   It seems from these entries (p. 79,* 125, 182, 209, 230, 265) that they lodged in the

* p. 79, Item the same daye paied to Johnson the mayster of the king*is* bargo for the Rent of the house where the henxe men lye xl s.

and they had "everyche of them an honest servaunt to keepe theyre chambre and harneys, and to aray hym in this courte whyles theyre maisters be present in courte." I suppose that when they grew up, some became Esquires, and then their teaching would prove of use, for

"These Esquiers of houshold of old [were] accustumed, wynter and sumer, in aftyrnoones and in eveninges, to drawe to lordes chambres within courte, there to kepe honest company aftyr theyre cunnynge, in talkyng of cronycles of Kings and of other polycyes, or in pypeyng or harpyng, synging, or other actes martialles, to help occupy the courte, and accompany straungers, tyll the tyme require of departing."

But that a higher station than an Esquier's was in store for some of these henchmen, may be known from the history of one of them. Thomas Howard, eldest son of Sir John Howard, knight (who was afterwards Duke of Norfolk, and killed at Bosworth Field), was among these henchmen or pages, 'enfauntes' six or more, of Edward IV.'s. He was made Duke of Norfolk for his splendid victory over the Scots at Flodden, and Anne Boleyn and Catherine Howard were his granddaughters. Among the 'othyr lerninges vertuous' taught

---

house of Johnson, the master of the king's barge, and that the rent of it was 40s. per annum. Observations on the word will be found in Spelman's *Etymol.*, Pegge's *Curialia*, from the Liber Niger, Edw. IV., Lodge's *Illustrations*, vol. i. p. 359, the *Northumberland Household Book*, Blount's *Glossary*."

The *Promptorium* has "Heyncemann (henchemanne) *Gerolocista, duorum generum (gerolocista),*" and Mr Way in his note says, "The pages of distinguished personages were called henxmen, as Spelman supposes, from Ger. *hengst*, a war-horse, or according to Bp. Percy, from their place being at the side or *haunch* of their lord." See the rest of Mr Way's note. He is a most provokingly careful editor. If ever you hit on a plum in your wanderings through other books you are sure to find it afterwards in one of Mr Way's notes when you bethink yourself of turning to the Promptorium.

In Lord Percy's Household (*North. H. Book*, p. 362) the Henchemen are mentioned next to the Earl's own sons and their tutor (?) in the list of "Persones that shall attende upon my Lorde at his Borde Daily, ande have no more but his Revercion Except Brede and Drynk."

My Lordes Secounde Son to serve as Kerver.
My Lordes Thurde Son as Sewer.
A Gentillman that shall attende upon my Lord's Eldest Son in the rewarde, and appoynted Bicause he shall allwayes be with my Lord's Sonnes for seynge the Orderynge of them.
My Lordes first *Hauneshman* to serve as Cupberer to my Lorde.
My Lords ij^de *Hanshman* to serve as Cupberer to my Lady.
See also p. 300, p. 254, The *Hansmen* to be at the fyndynge of my Lord, p. 47.

b 2

him at Edward's court was no doubt that of drawing, for we find that 'He was buried with much pomp at Thetford Abbey under a tomb designed by himself and master Clarke, master of the works at King's College, Cambridge, & Wassel a freemason of Bury S. Edmund's.' Cooper's *Ath. Cant.*, i. p. 29, col. 2.

The question of the social rank of these Bele Babees, children, and *Pueri* who stood at tables, opens up the whole subject of upper-class education in early times in England. It is a subject that, so far as I can find, has never yet been separately treated[1], and I therefore throw together such few notices as the kindness of friends[2] and my own chance grubbings have collected ; these as a sort of stopgap till the appearance of Mr Anstey's volume of early Oxford Statutes in the *Chronicles and Memorials*, a volume which will, I trust, give us a complete account of early education in our land. If it should not, I hope that Mr Quick will carry his pedagogic researches past Henry VIII.'s time, or that one of our own members will take the subject up. It is worthy of being thoroughly worked out. For convenience' sake, the notices I have mentioned are arranged under six heads :

1. Education in Nobles' houses.
2. At Home and at Private Tutors', p. xvii.
3. At English Universities, p. xxvi.
4. At Foreign Universities, p. xl.
5. At Monastic and Cathedral Schools, p. xli.
6. At Grammar Schools, p. lii.

One consideration should be premised, that manly exercises, manners and courtesy, music and singing, knowledge of the order of precedency of ranks, and ability to carve, were in early times more important than Latin and Philosophy. 'Aylmar þe kyng' gives these directions to Athelbrus, his steward, as to Horn's education :

---

[1] When writing this I had forgotten Warton's section on the Revival of Learning in England before and at the Reformation, *Hist. English Poetry*, v. iii. ed. 1840. It should be read by all who take an interest in the subject. Mr Bruce also refers to Kynaston's *Museum Minervæ*. P.S.—Mr Bullein and Mr Watts have since referred me to Henry, who has in each volume of his *History of England* a regular account of learning in England, the Colleges and Schools founded, and the learned men who flourished, in the period of which each volume treats. Had I seen these earlier I should not have got the following extracts together ; but as they are for the most part not in Henry, they will serve as a supplement to him.

[2] First of these is Mr Charles H. Pearson, then the Rev. Prof. Brewer, and Mr William Chappell.

Stiwarde, tak nu here
Mi fundlyng for to lere   228
Of þine mestere,
Of wude *and* of riuere ;
And tech him to harpe
Wiþ his nayles scharpe ;   232
Biuore me to kerue,
And of þe cupe serue ;
þu tech him of alle þe liste (craft, AS. *list*)
þat þu eure of wiste ;   236
[And] his feiren þou wise (mates thou teach)
Into oþere seruise.
Horn þu underuonge,
And tech him of harpe *and* songe.   240

King Horn, E. E. T. Soc., 1866, ed. Lumby, p. 7.[1]

So in Romances and Ballads of later date, we find

The child was taught great nurterye ;
a Master had him vnder his care,
& taught him *curtesie.*

Tryamore, in Bp. Percy's Folio MS. vol. ii. ed. 1867.

It was the worthy Lord of learen,
he was a lord of hie degree ;
he had noe more children but one sonne,
he sett him to schoole to learne *curtesie.*

Lord of Learne, Bp. Percy's Folio MS. vol. i. p. 182, ed. 1867.

Chaucer's Squire, as we know, at twenty years of age

hadde ben somtyme in chivachie,
In Flaundres, in Artoys, and in Picardie,
And born him wel, as in so litel space,
In hope to stonden in his lady grace . . .
Syngynge he was, or flowtynge, al the day . .
Wel cowde he sitte on hors, and wel cowde ryde.
He cowde songes wel make and endite,
Justne and eek daunce, and wel purtray and write . . .
Curteys he was, lowly, and servysable,
And carf beforn his fadur at the table.[2]

Which of these accomplishments would Cambridge or Oxford teach ?
Music alone. That, as Harrison says, was one of the Quadrivials,

---

[1] Mr Wm. Chappell gave me the reference.

[2] In the Romance of Blonde of Oxford, Jean of Dammartin is taken into the service of the Earl of Oxford as *escuier,* esquire. He waits at table on knights, squires, valets, boys and messengers. After table, the ladies keep him to talk French with them.

'arithmetike, musike, geometrie, and astronomie.' The Trivium was grammar, rhetoric and logic.

1. The chief places of education for the sons of our nobility and gentry were the houses of other nobles, and specially those of the Chancellors of our Kings, men not only able to read and write, talk Latin and French themselves, but in whose hands the Court patronage lay. As early as Henry the Second's time (A.D. 1154-62), if not before[1], this system prevailed. A friend notes that Fitz-Stephen says of Becket :

"The nobles of the realm of England and of neighbouring kingdoms used to send their sons to serve the Chancellor, whom he trained with honourable bringing-up and learning ; and when they had received the knight's belt, sent them back with honour to their fathers and kindred : some he used to keep. The king himself, his master, entrusted to him his son, the heir of the realm, to be brought up ; whom he had with him, with many sons of nobles of the same age, and their proper retinue and masters and proper servants in the honour due."—*Vita S. Thomæ*, pp. 189, 190, ed. Giles.

Roger de Hoveden, a Yorkshireman, who was a clerk or secretary to Henry the Second, says of Richard the Lionheart's unpopular chancellor, Longchamps the Bishop of Ely :

"All the sons of the nobles acted as his servants, with downcast looks, nor dared they to look upward towards the heavens unless it so happened that they were addressing him ; and if they attended to anything else they were pricked with a goad, which their lord held in his hand, fully mindful of his grandfather of pious memory, who, being of servile condition in the district of Beauvais, had, for his occupation, to guide the plough and whip up the oxen ; and who at length, to gain his liberty, fled to the Norman territory." (Riley's *Hoveden*, ii. 232, quoted in *The Cornhill Magazine*, vol. xv. p. 165.)[2]

---

[1] It was in part a principle of Anglo-Saxon society at the earliest period, and attaches itself to that other universal principle of fosterage. A Teuton chieftain always gathered round him a troop of young retainers in his hall who were voluntary servants, and they were, in fact, almost the only servants he would allow to touch his person. T. Wright.

[2] Compare Skelton's account of Wolsey's treatment of the Nobles, in *Why come ye not to Courte* (quoted in Ellis's *Letters*, v. ii. p. 3).

—" Our barons be so bolde, | For drede of the maystife cur,
Into a mouse hole they wold | For drede of the boucher's dog
Runne away and creep |
Like a mainy of sheep : |
Dare not look out a dur | " For and this curre do gnarl,
 | They must stande all afar

All Chancellors were not brutes of this kind, but we must remember that young people were subjected to rough treatment in early
days. Even so late as Henry VI.'s time, Agnes Paston sends to
London on the 28th of January, 1457, to pray the master of her son
of 15, that if the boy "hath not done well, nor will not amend," his
master Greenfield "will truly belash him till he will amend." And
of the same lady's treatment of her marriageable daughter, Elizabeth,
Clere writes on the 29th of June, 1454,

"She (the daughter) was never in so great sorrow as she is now-
a-days, for she may not speak with no man, whosoever come, ne not
may see nor speak with my man, nor with servants of her mother's,
but that she beareth her on hand otherwise than she meaneth ; and
she hath since Easter the most part been beaten once in the week
or twice, and sometimes twice on a day, and her head broken in two
or three places." (v. i. p. 50, col. 1, ed. 1840.)

The treatment of Lady Jane Grey by her parents was also very
severe, as she told Ascham, though she took it meekly, as her sweet
nature was :

"One of the greatest benefites that God ever gave me, is, that he
sent me so sharpe and severe Parentes, and so jentle a scholemaster.
For when I am in presence either of father or mother, whether I
speake, kepe silence, sit, stand, or go, eate, drinke, be merie or sad,
be sewyng, plaiyng, dauncing, or doing anie thing els, I must do it,
as it were, in soch weight, mesure, and number, even so perfitelie as
God made the world, or els I am so sharplie taunted, so cruellie
threatened, yea presentlie some tymes, with pinches, nippes, and
bobbes, and other waies which I will not name for the honor I beare
them, so without measure misordered, that I thinke my self in hell
till tyme cum that I must go to M. Elmer, who teacheth me so
jentlie, so pleasantlie, with soch faire allurementes to learning, that
I thinke all the tyme nothing whiles I am with him. And when I
am called from him, I fall on weeping."—*The Scholemaster*, ed. Mayor.

The inordinate beating[1] of boys by schoolmasters—whom he

To holde up their hand at the bar.
For all their noble bloude,
He pluckes them by the hood
And shakes them by the eare,
And bryngs them in such feare ;
He bayteth them lyke a beare,

Like an Ox or a Bul.
Their wittes, he sayth, are dul ;
He sayth they have no brayne
Their estate to maintaine :
And make to bowe the knee
Before his Majestie."

[1] Compare also the quotation from Piers Plowman's Crede, under No 5, p. xlv,
and Palsgrave, 1530 A.D., ' I mase, I stonysshe, *Je bestourne*. You mased the boye
so sore with beatyng that he coulde not speake a worde.' See a gross instance of

calls in different places 'sharp, fond, & lewd'[1]—Ascham denounces strongly in the first book of his *Scholemaster*, and he contrasts their folly in beating into their scholars the hatred of learning with the practice of the wise riders who by gentle allurements breed them up in the love of riding. Indeed, the origin of his book was Sir Wm. Cecil's saying to him " I have strange news brought me this morning, that divers scholars of Eton be run away from the school for fear of beating."

- Sir Peter Carew, says Mr Froude, being rather a troublesome boy, was chained in the Haccombe dog-kennel till he ran away from it.

But to return to the training of young men in nobles' houses. I take the following from Fiddes's Appendix to his Life of Wolsey :

John de Athon, upon the Constitutions of *Othobon*, *tit.* 23, in respect to the Goods of such who dyed intestate, and upon the Word *Burones*, has the following Passage concerning *Grodsted* Bishop of *Lincoln*[2] (who died 9th Oct., 1253),—

"Robert surnamed Grodsted of holy memory, late Bishop of Lincoln, when King Henry asked him, as if in wonder, where he learnt the Nurture in which he had instructed the sons of nobles (&) peers of the Realm, whom he kept about him as pages (*domisellos*[3]), —since he was not descended from a noble lineage, but from humble (parents)—is said to have answered fearlessly, 'In the house or guest-

cruelty cited from Erasmus's Letters, by Staunton, in his *Great Schools of England*, p. 179-80.

[1] "And therfore do I the more lament that soch [hard] wittes commonlie be either kepte from learning by fond fathers, or *bet from learning by lewde schole-masters*," ed. Mayor, p. 19. But Ascham reproves parents for paying their masters so badly: " it is pitie, that commonlie more care is had, yea and that emonges verie wise men, to finde out rather a cunnynge man for their horse than a cunnyng man for their children. They say nay in worde, but they do so in decde. For, to the one they will gladlie give a stipend of 200. Crounes by yeare, and loth to offer to the other, 200. shillinges. God, that sitteth in heauen, laugheth their choice to skorne, and rewardeth their liberalitie as it should : for he suffereth them to have tame and well ordered horse, but wilde and unfortunate Children." *Ib.* p. 20.

[2-2] *Sanctæ memoriæ* Robertum *Cognominatum* Grodsted *dudum* Lincolniendem *Episcopum, Regi* Henrico *quasi admirando, cum interrogavit, ubi Noraturam didicit, quâ Filios Nobilium Procerum Regni, quos secum habuit Domisellos, instruxerat, cum non de nobili prosapia, sed de simplicibus traxisset Originem, fertur intrepide respon-disse, In Domo seu Hospitio Majorum Regum quam sit Rex Angliæ ; Quia Regum,* David, Salomonis, & *aliorum, vivendi morem didicerat ex Intelligentia scripturarum.*

[3] DOMICELLUS, Domnicellus, diminutivum a *Domnus.* Gloss. antiquæ MSS. : *Heriles, Domini minores, quod possumus aliter dicere Domnicelli,* Ugutio : *Domicelli et Domicellæ dicuntur, quando pulchri juvenes magnatum sunt sicut servientes.* Sic porro primitus appellabant magnatum, atque adeo Regum filios. Du Cange.

chambers of greater kings than the King of England'; because he had learnt from understanding the scriptures the manner of life of David, Solomon, & other Kings [2]."

Reyner, in his *Apostol. Bened.* from *Saunders* acquaints us, that the Sons of the Nobility were placed with *Whiting* Abbot of *Glastenbury* for their Education, who was contemporary with the Cardinal, and which Method of Education was continued for some Time afterward.

There is in the Custody of the present Earl of *Stafford*, a Nobleman of the greatest Humanity and Goodness, an Original of Instructions, by the Earl of *Arundell*, written in the Year 1620, for the Benefit of his younger Son, the Earl of *Stafford's* Grandfather, under this Title ;

> *Instructions for you my Son* William, *how to behave your self at* Norwich.

In these Instructions is the following paragraph, " You shall in all Things reverence honour and obey my Lord Bishop of *Norwich*, as you would do any of your Parents, esteeminge whatsoever He shall tell or Command you, as if your Grandmother of *Arundell*, your Mother, or my self, should say it ; and in all things esteem your self as my Lord's Page ; a breeding which youths of my house far superior to you were accustomed unto, as my Grandfather of *Norfolk*, and his Brother my good Uncle of *Northampton* were both bred as Pages with Bishopps, *&c.* "

Sir Thomas More, who was born in 1480, was brought up in the house of Cardinal Morton. Roper says that he was

" received into the house of the right reverend, wise, and learned prelate Cardinal Morton, where, though he was young of years, yet would he at Christmas-tide suddenly sometimes step in among the players, and never studying for the matter make a part of his own there presently among them, which made the lookers on more sport than all the players beside. In whose wit and towardness the Cardinal much delighting would say of him unto the nobles that divers times dined with him, *This child here waiting at the table, whosoever shall live to see it, will prove a marvellous man.* Whereupon for his better furtherance in learning he placed him at Oxford, &c." (Roper's *Life of More*, ed. Singer, 1822, p. 3.)

Cresacre More in his *Life of More* (ed. 1828, p. 17) states the same thing more fully, and gives the remark of the Cardinal more accurately, thus :—" that that boy there waiting *on him*, whoever should live to see it, would prove a marvellous rare man."[1]

Through Wolsey's household, says Professor Brewer, almost all the

---

[1] Mr Bruce sends me the More extracts.

Officials of Henry the Eighth's time passed.   Cavendish, in his Life
of Wolsey (vol. i. p. 38, ed. Singer, 1825) says of the Cardinal,
" And at meals, there was continually in his chamber a board kept
for his Chamberlains, and Gentlemen Ushers, having with them *a
mess of the young Lords*, and another for gentlemen." Among these
young Lords, we learn at p. 57, was

" my Lord Percy, the son and heir of the Earl of Northumberland, [who] then attended upon the Lord Cardinal, and was also his
servitor ; and when it chanced the Lord Cardinal at any time to repair
to the court, the Lord Percy would then resort for his pastime unto
the queen's chamber, and there would fall in dalliance among the
queen's maidens, being at the last more conversant with Mistress
Anne Boleyn than with any other ; so that there grew such a secret
love between them that, at length they were insured together, intend-
ing to marry [1]."

Among the persons daily attendant upon Wolsey in his house,
down-lying and up-rising, Cavendish enumerates "of Lords nine or
ten, who had each of them allowed two servants ; and the Earl of
Derby had allowed 'five men" (p. 36-7).   On this Singer prints a note,
which looks like a guess, signed *Growe*, " Those Lords that were
placed in the great and privy chambers were *Wards*, and as such
paid for their board and education."   It will be seen below that he had
a particular officer called " Instructor of his Wards" (*Cavendish*,
p. 38, l. 2).   Why I suppose the note to be a guess is, because at p.
33 Cavendish has stated that Wolsey "had also a great number
daily attending upon him, both of noblemen and worthy gentlemen,
of great estimation and possessions,—with no small number of the
tallest yeomen that he could get in all his realm ; in so much that
well was that nobleman and gentleman that might prefer any tall and
comely yeoman unto his service."

In the household of the Earl of Northumberland in 1511 were
". . yong gentlemen at their fryndes fynding,[2] in my lords house for

---

[1] How Wolsey broke off the *insurance* is very well told.   Mistress Anne was
" sent home again to her father for a season ; *whereat she smoked* " *;* but she " was
revoked unto the Court," and " after she knew the king's pleasure and the great
love that he bare her *in the bottom of his stomach*, then she began to look very hault
and stout, having all manner of jewels or rich apparel that might be gotten with
money " (p. 67).

[2] Under the heading " Gentylmen of Houshold, viz. Kervers, Sewars, Cupberers, and Gentillmen Waiters " in the *North. Household Books*, p. 40, we find

the hoole yere" and "Haunsmen ande Yong Gentlemen at thir
Fryndes fynding v[j] (As to say, Hanshmen iij. And Yong Gentlemen iij" p. 254,) no doubt for the purpose of learning manners, &c.
And that such youths would be found in the house of every noble of
importance I believe, for as Walter Mapes (? ab. 1160-90 A.D.) says
of the great nobles, in his poem *De diversis ordinibus hominum,* the
example of manners goes out from their houses, *Exemplar morum
domibus procedit eorum.* That these houses were in some instances
only the finishing schools for our well-born young men after previous
teaching at home and at College is possible (though the cases of Sir
Thomas More and Ascham are exactly the other way), but the Lord
Percy last named had a schoolmaster in his house, "The Maister of
Graimer j", p. 254 ; "Lyverays for the Maister of Gramer [1] in
Housholde : Item Half a Loof of Houshold Breide, a Pottell of Beere,
and two White Lyghts," p. 97. "Every Scolemaister techyng
Grammer in the Hous C *s.*" (p. 47, 51). Edward IV.'s henxmen were
taught grammar ; and if the Pastons are to be taken as a type of their
class, our nobles and gentry at the end of the 15th century must
have been able to read and write freely. Chaucer's Squire could
write, and though the custom of sealing deeds and not signing them
prevailed, more or less, till Henry VIII.'s time, it is doubtful whether
this implied inability of the sealers to write. Mr Chappell says that
in Henry VIII.'s time half our nobility were then writing ballads.
Still, the bad spelling and grammar of most of the letters up to that
period, and the general ignorance of our upper classes were, says
Professor Brewer, the reason why the whole government of the
country was in the hands of ecclesiastics. Even in Henry the Eighth's

Item, Gentillmen in Housholde ix, Viz. ij Carvers for my Loords Boorde, and a
Servant bitwixt theym both, *except that be at their frendis fyndyng,* and than ather
of theym to have a Servant.—Two Sewars for my Lordis Boorde, and a Servant
bitwixt theym, *except they be at their Friendis fyndynge,* and than ather of theym
to have a Servant.—ij Cupberers for my Lorde and my Lady, and a Servant allowed
bitwixt theym, *except they be at their Frendis fyndynge,* And than ather of theym to
have a Servant allowid.
Under the next heading "My Lordis Hansmen at the fyndynge of my Lorde,
and Yonge Gentyllmen *at there Frendys fyndynge,*" is
Item, my Lordis Hansmen iij. Yonge Gentyllmen in Houshold *at their Frendis
fyndynge* ij = v.
[1] Grammar usually means Latin. T. Wright.

time, Sir Thomas Boleyn is said to have been the only noble at Court who could speak French with any degree of fluency, and so was learned enough to be sent on an embassy abroad. But this may be questioned. Yet Wolsey, speaking to his Lord Chamberlain and Comptroller when they

"showed him that it seemed to them there should be some noblemen and strangers [Henry VIII. and his courtiers masked] arrived at his bridge, as ambassadors from some foreign prince. With that, quoth the Cardinal, 'I shall desire you, *because ye can speak French*, to take the pains to go down into the hall to encounter and to receive them, according to their estates, and to conduct them into this chamber' (*Cavendish*, p. 51). Then spake my Lord Chamberlain unto them *in French*, declaring my Lord Cardinal's mind (p. 53)."

The general[1] opinion of our gentry as to the study of Letters, before and about 1500 A.D., is probably well represented by the opinion of one of them stated by Pace, in his Prefatory Letter to Colet, prefixed to the former's *De Fructu*[2].

[1] The exceptions must have been many and marked.

[2] *Richardi Pacei, invictissimi Regis Angliæ primarii Secretarii, eiusque apud Elvetios Oratoris, De Fructu qui ex Doctrinæ percipitur, Liber.*
Colophon. *Basileae apud Io. Frobenium, mense* VIII.*bri. an.* M.D.XVII.
Restat ut iam tibi explicem, quid me moueat ad libellum hoc titulo conscribendum *et* publicandu*m*. Quu*m* duobus annis plus minus iam præteritis, ex Romana urbe in patriam redijssem, inter-fui cuida*m* conuiuio multis incognitus. Vbi quu*m* satis fuisset potatum, unus, nescio quis, ex conuiuis, non imprudens, ut ex uerbis uultuqu*e* co'nijcere licuit, cœpit mentionem facere de liberis suis bene instituendis. Et primum omniu*m*, bonu*m* præceptorem illis sibi quærendu*m*, & scholam omnino frequentanda*m* censuit. Aderat forte unus ex his, quos nos generosos uocamus, & qui semper cornu aliquod a tergo pende*n*s gestant, acsi etia*m* inter prandendum uenarentur. Is audita literarum laude, percitus repentina ira, furibundus prorupit in hæc uerba. Quid nugaris, inquit, amice? abeant in malam rem ista stultæ literæ, omnes docti sunt me*n*dici, etia*m* Erasmus ille doctissimus (ut audio) pauper est, & in quadam sua epistola uocat τηυ καράρατου πευιαυ uxorem suam, id est, execrandam paupertatem, & uehementer conqueritur se son posse illam humeris suis usqu*e* in βαθυκήτεα πόυτου, id est, profundum mare excutere. (Corpus dei iuro) uolo filius meus pendeat potius, qua*m* literis studeat. Decet eni*m* generosorum filios,*f*apto inflare cornu, perite uenari, accipitrem pulchre gestare & educare. Studia uero literarum, rusticorum filiis sunt relinquenda. Hic ego cohibere me no*n* potui, quin aliqu*i*d homini loquacissimo, in defensionem bonarum literarum, respo*n*derem. Non uideris, inqua*m*, mihi bono uir recte sentire, nam si ueniret ad regem aliqu*i*s uir exterus, quales sunt principu*m* oratores, & ei dandu*m* esset responsum, filius tuus sic ut tu uis, institutus, inflaret du*n*taxat cornu, & rusticoru*m* filij docti, ad respondendu*m* uocarentu*r*, ac filio tuo uenatori uel aucupi longe anteponerentu*r*, & sua crudita

It remains that I now explain to you what moves me to compile — and publish a treatise with this title. When, two years ago, more or less, I had returned to my native land from the city of Rome, I was present at a certain feast, a stranger to many ; where, when enough had been drunk, one or other of the guests—no fool, as one might infer from his words and countenance—began to talk of educating his children well.- And, first of all, he thought that he must search out a good teacher for them, and that they should at any rate attend school. There happened to be present one of those whom we call gentle-men (*generosos*), and who always carry some horn hanging at their backs, as though they would hunt during dinner. He, hearing letters praised, roused with sudden anger, burst out furiously with these words. "Why do you talk nonsense, friend ? " he said ; " A curse on those stupid letters ! all learned men are beggars : even Erasmus, the most learned of all, is a beggar (as I hear), and in a certain letter of his calls τὴν κατάρατον πενίαν (that is, execrable poverty) his wife, and vehemently complains that he cannot shake her off his shoulders right into βαθυκήτεα πόντον, that is, into the deep sea. I swear by God's body I'd rather that my son should hang than study letters. For it becomes the sons of gentlemen to blow the horn nicely (*apte*), to hunt skilfully, and elegantly carry and train a hawk. But the study of letters should be left to the sons of rustics." At this point I could not restrain myself from answering something to this most talkative man, in defence of good letters. " You do not seem to me, good man," I said, " to think rightly. For if any foreigner were to come to the king, such as the ambassadors (*oratores*) of princes are, and an answer had to be given to him, your son, if he were educated as you wish, could only blow his horn, and the learned sons of rustics would be called to answer, and would be far preferred to your hunter or fowler son ; and they, enjoying their learned liberty, would say to your face, ' We prefer to be learned, and, thanks to our learning, no fools, than boast of our fool-like nobility. ' " Then he upon this, looking round, said, " Who is this person that is talking like this ? I don't know the fellow." And when some one whispered in his ear who I was, he muttered something or other in a low voice to himself ; and finding a fool to listen to him, he then caught hold of a cup of wine. And when he

usi libertate, tibi in faciem dicerent, Nos malumus docti esse, & per doctrinam non imprudentes, quam stulta gloriari nobilitate. Tum ille hincinde circumspiciens, Quis est iste, inquit, qui hæc loquitur ? hominem non cognosco. Et quum diceretur in aurem ei quisnam essem, nescio quid submissa uoce sibimet susurrans, & stulto usus auditore, illico arripuit uini poculum. Et quum nihil haberet respondendum, cœpit bibere, & in alia sermonem transferre. Et sic me liberauit, non Apollo, ut Horatium a garrulo, sed Bacchus a uesani hominis disputatione, quam diutius longe duraturam uehementer timebam.

Professor Brewer gives me the reference.

could get nothing to answer, he began to drink, and change the conversation to other things. And thus I was freed from the disputing of this mad fellow,—which I was dreadfully afraid would have lasted a long time,—not by Apollo, like Horace was from his babbler, but by Bacchus.

On the general subject it should be noted that Fleta mentions nothing about boarders or apprentices in his account of household economy ; nor does the *Liber Contrarotulatoris Garderobæ Edw. I^{mi}* mention any young noblemen as part of the King's household. That among tradesmen in later times, putting out their children in other houses, and apprenticeships, were the rule, we know from many statements and allusions in our literature, and "The Italian Relation of England" (temp. Hen. VII.) mentions that the Duke of Suffolk was boarded out to a rich old widow, who persuaded him to marry her (p. 27). It also says

The want of affection in the English is strongly manifested towards their children ; for after having kept them at home till they arrive at the age of 7 or 9 years at the utmost, they put them out, both males and females, to hard service in the houses of other people, binding them generally for another 7 or 9 years. And these are called apprentices, and during that time they perform all the most menial offices ; and few are born who are exempted from this fate, for every one, however rich he may be, sends away his children into the houses of others, whilst he, in return, receives those of strangers into his own. And on inquiring their reason for this severity, they answered that they did it in order that their children might learn better manners. But I, for my part, believe that they do it because they like to enjoy all their comforts themselves, and that they are better served by strangers than they would be by their own children. Besides which, the English being great epicures, and very avaricious by nature, indulge in the most delicate fare themselves and give their household the coarsest bread, and beer, and cold meat baked on Sunday for the week, which, however, they allow them in great abundance. That if they had their own children at home, they would be obliged to give them the same food they made use of for themselves. That if the English sent their children away from home to learn virtue and good manners, and took them back again when their apprenticeship was over, they might, perhaps, be excused ; but they never return, for the girls are settled by their patrons, and the boys make the best marriages they can, and, assisted by their patrons, not by their fathers, they also open a house and strive diligently by this means to make some fortune for themselves ; whence it proceeds that, having no hope of their paternal inheritance, that all become so greedy of gain that they feel no shame in asking, almost "for the love of God," for the smallest sums of money; and to this it may be attributed, that there is no injury that can be committed against the lower orders of the English, that may not be atoned for by money.— *A Relation of the Island of England* (Camden Society, 1847), pp. 24-6.

"This evidently refers to tradesmen.[1] The note by the Editor[2] however says it was the case with the children of the first nobility, and gives the terms for the Duke of Buckingham's children with Mrs Hexstall. The document only shows that Mrs Hexstall boarded them by contract 'during the time of absence of my Lord and my Ladie.'"

The Earl of Essex says in a letter to Lord Burleigh, 1576, printed in Murdin's *State Papers*, p. 301-2.

"Neverthelesse, uppon the assured Confidence, that your love to me shall dissend to my Childrenne, and that your Lordship will declare yourself a Frend to me, both alive and dead, I have willed Mr *Waterhouse* to shew unto you how you may with Honor and Equity do good to my Sonne *Hereford*, and how to bind him with perpetual Frendship to you and your House. And to the Ende I wold have his Love towardes those which are dissended from you spring up and increase with his Yeares, I have wished his Education to be in your Houschold, though the same had not bene allotted to your Lordship as Master of the Wardes; and that the whole Tyme, which he shold spend in *England* in his Minority, might be devided in Attendance uppon my Lord *Chamberlayne* and you, to the End, that as he might frame himself to the Example of my Lord of *Sussex* in all the Actions of his Life, tending either to the Warres, or to the Institution of a Nobleman, so that he might also reverence your Lordship for your Wisdome and Gravyty, and lay up your Counsells and Advises in the Treasury of his Hart."

That girls, as well as boys, were sent out to noblemen's houses for their education, is evident from Margaret Paston's letter of the 3rd of April, 1469, to Sir John Paston, " Also I would ye should purvey for your sister [? Margery] to be with my Lady of Oxford, or with, my Lady of Bedford, or in some other worshipful place whereas ye think best, and I will help to her finding, for we be either of us, weary of other." Alice Crane's Letter, in the Paston Letters, v. i. p.

---

[1] As to agricultural labourers and their children A.D. 1388-1406, see below, p. xlvi.

[2] Readers will find it advisable to verify for themselves some of the statements in this Editor's notes, &c.

35, ed. 1840, also supports this view, as does Sir John Heveningham's
to Margaret Paston, asking her to take his cousin Anneys Loveday
for some time as a boarder till a mistress could be found for her. "If
that it please you to have her with you to into the time that a
mistress may be purveyed for her, I pray you thereof, and I shall
content you for her board that ye shall be well pleased." Similarly
Anne Boleyn and her sister were sent to Margaret of Savoy, aunt of
Charles V., who lived at Brussels, to learn courtesy, &c., says Prof.
Brewer. Sir Roger Twysden says that Anne was "Not above seven
yeares of age, Anno 1514," when she went abroad. He adds :

"It should seeme by some that she served three in France suc-
cessively; Mary of England maryed to Lewis the twelfth, an. 1514,
with whome she went out of England, but Lewis dying the first of
January following, and that Queene (being) to returne home, sooner
than either Sir Thomas Bullen or some other of her frendes liked she
should, she was preferred to Clauda, daughter to Lewis XII. and
wife to Francis I. then Queene (it is likely upon the commendation
of Mary the Dowager), who not long after dying, an. 1524, not yet
weary of France she went to live with Marguerite, Dutchess of
Alançon and Berry, a Lady much commended for her favor towards
good letters, but never enough for the Protestant religion then in the
infancy—from her, if I am not deceived, she first learnt the grounds
of the Protestant religion; so that England may seem to owe some
part of her happyness derived from that Lady." (Twysden's Notes
quoted by Singer in his ed. of Cavendish's Life of Wolsey, 1825, p.
57.)

As Henry VIII. fell in love with his wife's maid of honour,—
"began to kindle the brand of amours" at the light of Anne Boleyn's
beauty, "her excellent gesture and behaviour,"—so we find in later
times rich young men became enamoured of poor young women stay-
ing in the same house with them. Mr Bruce sends me an instance :

"the young lady was niece, you will perceive, to a well-beneficed
clergyman, and a thriving gentleman well-advanced in the public
service. She had lost her mother, and her father was in debt and
difficulties. She was therefore placed by the influence of her uncles
in a well-known family in Wiltshire."

State Papers. Dom. Car. I, Vol. ccclii. No. 29. Dr Matthew
Nicholas, afterwards Dean of St Paul's, to Edward Nicholas, Clerk
of the Council, and afterwards Secretary of State. Dated, West
Dean, April 4, 1637.

"I have spoken with Miss Evelyn since I wrote last unto you,
and enquired of her the cause which moued her to displace my coson

Hunton. She told me much accordinge to what she had sayd unto my coson Hunton, with this addition, that she had respect in it as well unto her good as her owne convenience, for hauinge nowe noe employment for her but her needle, she founde that sittinge still at her worke made her sickly, and therefore thought she might doe better in another seruice where she might haue the orderinge of an huswifely charge, for which (she told me) she had made her very able. I expressed myselfe tender of the disgrace which would lay uppon my coson in beinge displaced in such a manner by warninge giuen, wherof whatsoeuer were the cause, it would be imagined by all that knowe it not, to be in her ill carriage, and wished she had done me that fauour as to haue acquainted me with her intents in such time as I might haue taken some course to haue disposed of her before it had bin knowne that she was to leaue her: she slubbered it ouer with a slight excuse that she had acquainted my wife . . . . but for my satisfaction she told me that she would be as mindfull of her when God should call her as if she were with her, and in testimony of her good likinge of her seruice she would allowe her forty shillings yearly towarde her maintainance as longe as herself should liue. I am soe well acquainted with what she hath as yet disposed to her by will, and soe little value forty shillings to my coson Hunton's credit, as I gaue her noe thankes. Mr Downes (I heare) is sent for home by his father with an intent to keepe him with him, but I doe imagine that when my coson Hunton shall be other where disposed off, he shall returne; for my conceit is stronge that the feare of his beinge match'd to his disadvantage, who was placed with Mr Evelyn a youth to be bred for his preferment, hath caused this alteration; howsoever there be noe wordes made of it. I confess that when I have bin told of the good will that was obserued betweene my coson Hunton and Mr Downes, I did put it by with my coson Huntons protestation to the contrary, and was willinge by that neglect to have suffered it to have come to pass (if it mought have bin) because I thought it would haue bin to her aduantage, but nowe that the busines is come to this issue (as whatsoeuer be pretended I am confident this is the cause of my cosons partinge) I begin to quæstion my discretion. . . . Good brother, let me haue your aduise what to do."

2. *Home and Private Education.* Of these, more or less must have been going on all over England, by private tutors at home, or in the houses of the latter. "In five years (after my baptism) I was handed over by my father to Siward, a noble priest, to be trained in letters, to whose mastery I was subdued during five years learning the first rudiments. But in the eleventh year of my age I was given up by my own father for the love of God, and destined to enter the service of the eternal King."—*Orderic*, vol. ii. p. 301, ed. Prevost.

c

From Adam de Marisco's Letters, 53, we find that Henry and Almeric, the eldest and youngest sons of the Earl of Montfort, were put under Grosseteste for tuition, he being then a Bishop. At Paris, John of Salisbury (who died in 1180) gained a living by teaching the sons of noblemen,—(*instruendos susceperam,* ? took them in to board). —*Metalogicus,* lib. 11, c. 10.

Henry of Huntingdon says, " Richard, the king's (Henry I.'s) bastard son, was honourably brought up (*festive nutritus*) by our Bishop Robert (Blote of Lincoln), and duly reverenced by me and others in the same household I lived in."—*Anglia Sacra,* vol. ii. p. 696. Giraldus Cambrensis speaks of beating his *coætanei et conscolares terræ suæ,* of being reproved for idleness by his uncle, the Bishop of St David's, and of being constantly chaffed by two of his uncle's chaplains, who used to decline *durus* and *stultus* to him. Also he alludes to the rod. Probably there was some sort of school at either Pembroke or St David's.—*De Rebus a se Gestis,* lib. 1, c. 2.[1]

The Statutes of a Gild of young Scholars formed to burn lights in honour of some saint or other, and to help one another in sickness, old age, and to burial, will be printed for us by Mr Toulmin Smith in the Early English Text Society's books this year.

Under this head of Private Tuition we may class the houses of Abbots, where boys of good birth were educated. In his History of English Poetry, section 36, vol. iii. p. 9, ed. 1840, Warton says :

" It appears to have been customary for the governors of the most considerable convents, especially those that were honoured with the mitre, to receive into their own private lodgings the sons of the principal families of the neighbourhood for education. About the year 1450, Thomas Bromele, abbot of the mitred monastery of Hyde near Winchester, entertained in his own abbatial house within that monastery eight young gentlemen, or *gentiles pueri,* who were placed there for the purpose of literary instruction, and constantly dined at the abbot's table. I will not scruple to give the original words, which are more particular and expressive, of the obscure record which preserves this curious anecdote of monastic life. ' *Pro octo gentilibus pueris apud dominum abbatem studii causa perhendinantibus, et ad mensam domini victitantibus, cum garcionibus suis ipsos comitantibus, hoc anno, xviil. ixs. Capiendo pro*[2] . . .*"* This, by the way,

---

[1] The foregoing three extracts are sent me by a friend.

[2] From a fragment of the Computus Camerarii Abbat. Hidens. in Archiv. Wulves. apud Winton. ut supr. (? Hist. Reg. Angl. edit. Hearne, p. 74.)

was more extraordinary, as William of Wykeham's celebrated
seminary was so near. And this seems to have been an established
practice of the abbot of Glastonbury, "whose apartment in the
abbey was a kind of well-disciplined court, where the sons of noblemen and young gentlemen were wont to be sent for virtuous education, who returned thence home excellently accomplished.[1]" Richard
Whiting, the last abbot of Glastonbury, who was cruelly executed by
the king, during the course of his government educated near three
hundred ingenuous youths, who constituted a part of his family;
beside many others whom he liberally supported at the universities.[2]
Whitgift, the most excellent and learned archbishop of Canterbury
in the reign of Queen Elizabeth, was educated under Robert Whitgift
his uncle, abbot of the Augustine monastery of black canons at
Wellhow in Lincolnshire, "who," says Strype "had several other
young gentlemen under his care for education." (Strype's Whitgift,
v. i. ch. i. p. 3.)

Of Lydgate—about 1420-30 A.D. I suppose—Prof. Morley says in
his *English Writers*, vol. ii. Pt. I. p. 423 :

" After studying at Oxford, Paris, and Padua, and after mastering
with special delight the writings of such poets as Dante, Boccaccio,
and Alain Chartier, Lydgate opened at his monastery of Bury St
Edmund's a school of rhetoric in which he taught young nobles
literature and the art of versifying !"

Richard Pace says in his *De Fructu*, 1517:

"Now the learning of music too demands its place, especially
from me whom it distinguished when a boy amongst boys. For
Thomas Langton, bishop of Winchester (the predecessor of him who is
now living), whose secretary I was, when he had marked that I was
making a proficiency in music far beyond my age (as himself—per-
chance from his too great affection for me—would point out and
repeatedly say), 'The talent of this lad,' he said, 'is born for greater
things,' and a few days afterwards he sent me, to pursue the study of
literature, into Italy, to the school at Padua, which then was at its
greatest prime, and benevolently supplied the annual expenses, as he
showed wonderful favour to all men of letters, and in his day played
the part of a second Mecaenas, well remembering (as he ofttimes said)
that he had been advanced to the episcopal dignity on account of
his learning. For he had gained, with the highest commendation, the
distinctions of each law[3] (as they say now-a-days). Also he so
highly prized the study of Humanity[4] that he had boys and youths

[1] Hist. and Antiq. of Glastonbury. Oxon. 1722, 8vo, p. 98.
[2] Reyner, Apostolat. Benedict. Tract. 1, sect. ii. p. 224. Sanders de Schism.
page 176.
[3] *utriusque juris*, Canon and Civil.
[4] *Lit. humaniores*. Latin is still called so in Scotch, and French (I think),
universities. J. W. Hales.

instructed in it at a school in his house; And he was vastly
delighted to hear the scholars repeat to him at night the lessons
given them by the teacher during the day. In this competition he
who had borne himself notably went away with a present of something suitable to his character, and with commendation expressed in
the most refined language; for that excellent governor had ever in
his mouth the maxim that merit grows with praise."[1]

Palsgrave in 1530 speaks of "maister Petrus Vallensys, scole
maister to his [Charles, Duke of Suffolk's] excellent yong sonne the
Erle of Lyncolne."

Roger Ascham, author of the *Scholemaster*, &c., born in 1515,

" was received at a very youthful age into the family of Sir
Antony Wingfield, who furnished money for his education, and
placed Roger, together with his own sons, under a tutor whose
name was Bond. The boy had by nature a taste for books, and
showed his good taste by reading English in preference to Latin,
with wonderful eagerness. This was the more remarkable from the
fact that Latin was still the language of literature, and it is not
likely that the few English books written at that time were at all
largely spread abroad in places far away from the Universities and
Cathedral towns. In or about the year 1530, Mr Bond the domestic
tutor resigned the charge of young Roger, who was now about fifteen
years old, and by the advice and pecuniary aid of his kind patron
Sir Antony, he was enabled to enter St John's College, Cambridge,
at that time the most famous seminary of learning in all England . .
he took his bachelor's degree in 1531, Feb. 18, in the 18th year of
his age [" being a boy, new bachelor of art," he says himself,] a time
of life at which it is now more common to enter the University than
to take a degree, but which, according to the modes of education

---

[1] (Pace *de Fructu*, p. 27.) Exigit iam suum musica quoque doctrina locum, a me
praesertim, quem puerum inter pueros illustravit. Nam Thomas Langton Vyntoni-
ensis episcopus, decessor huius qui nunc [1517 A.D.] uiuit, cui eram a manu
minister, quum notasset me longe supra aetatem (ut ipse nimis fortasse amans mei
iudicabat, & dictitabat) in musicis proficere, Huius, inquit, pueri ingenium ad
maiora natum est. & paucos post dies in Italiam ad Patauinum gymnasium, quod
tunc florentissimum erat, ad bonas literas discendas me misit, annuasque impensas
benigne suppeditauit, ut omnibus literatis mirifice fauebat, & aetate sua alterum
Mcccnatem agebat, probe memor (ut frequenter dictitabat) sese doctrinae causa ad
episcopalem dignitatem prouectum. Adeptus enim fuerat per summam laudem,
utriusque iuris (ut nunc loquuntur) insignia. Item humaniores literas tanti aesti-
mabat, ut domestica schola pueros & iuuenes illis erudiendos curarit. Et summo-
pere oblectabatur audire scholasticos dictata interdiu a praeceptore, sibi nocta
reddere. In quo certamine qui praeclare se gesserat, is aliqua re personae suae
accommodata, donatus abibat, & humanissimis uerbis laudatus. Habebet enim
semper in ore ille optimus Praesul, uirtutem laudatam crescere.

then in use, was not thought premature. On the 23rd of March following, he was elected fellow of the College." Giles's Life of Ascham, Works, vol. i. p. xi-xiv.

Dr Clement and his wife were brought up in Sir T. More's house. Clement was taken from St Paul's school, London, appointed tutor to More's children, and afterwards to his daughter Margaret, p. 402, col. 1.

What a young nobleman learnt in Henry the Eighth's time may be gathered from the following extracts (partly given by Mr Froude, Hist., v. i. p. 39-40) from the letters of young Gregory Cromwell's tutor, to his father, the Earl of Essex, the King's Chief Secretary.

"The order of his studie, as the houres lymyted for the Frenche tongue, writinge, plaienge att weapons, castinge of accomptes, pastimes of instruments, and suche others, hath bene devised and directed by the prudent wisdome of Mr Southwell; who with a ffatherly zeale and amitie muche desiringe to have hime a sonne worthy suche parents, ceasseth not aswell concerninge all other things for hime mete and necessary, as also in lerninge, t'expresse his tendre love and affection towardes hime, serchinge by all meanes possible howe he may moste proffitte, dailie heringe hime to rede sumwhatt in thenglishe tongue, and advertisenge hime of the naturell and true kynde of pronuntiacon therof, expoundinge also and declaringe the etimologie and native signification of suche wordes as we have borowed of the Latines or Frenche menne, not evyn so comonly used in our quotidiene speche. Mr Cheney and Mr Charles in lyke wise endevoireth and emploieth themselves, accompanienge Mr Gregory in lerninge, amonge whome ther is a perpetuall contention, strife, and conflicte, and in maner of an honest envie who shall do beste, not oonlie in the ffrenche tongue (wherin Mr Vallence after a wonderesly compendious, facile, prompte, and redy waye, nott withoute painfull delegence and laborious industrie doth enstructe them) but also in writynge, playenge att weapons, and all other theire exercises, so that if continuance in this bihalf may take place, whereas the laste Diana, this shall (I truste) be consecrated to Apollo and the Muses, to theire no small profecte and your good contentation and pleasure. And thus I beseche the Lord to have you in his moste gratious tuition.

At Reisinge in Norff[olk] the last daie of Aprill.
Your faithfull and most bounden servaunte
HENRY DOWES.
To his right honorable maister Mr Thomas Crumwell chief Secretary vnto the King's Maiestie."
Ellis, *Original Letters.* Series I. vol. i. p. 341-3.

The next Letter gives further details of Gregory's studies—

" But forcause somer was spente in the servyce of the wylde goddes, it is so moche to be regarded after what fashion yeouth is educate and browght upp, in whiche tyme that that is lerned (for the moste parte) will nott all holelie be forgotten in the older yeres, I thinke it my dutie to asserteyne yor Maistershippe how he spendith his tyme. . . . . . And firste, after he hath herde Masse he taketh a lecture of a Diologe of Erasmus Colloquium, called Pietas Puerilis, whereinne is described a veray picture of oone that sholde be vertu-ouselie brought upp ; and forcause it is so necessary for hime, I do not onelie cause him to rede it over, but also to practise the preceptes of the same, and I have also translated it into Englishe, so that he may conferre theime both to-githers, whereof (as lerned men affirme) cometh no smalle profecte[1] . . after that, he exerciseth his hande in writing one or two houres, and redith uppon Fabian's Chronicle as longe ; the residue of the day he doth spende uppon the lute and virginalls.   When he rideth (as he doth very ofte) I tell hime by the way some historie of the Romanes or the Greekes, whiche I cause him to reherse agayn in a tale.   For his recreation he useth to hawke and hunte, and shote in his long bowe, which frameth and succedeth so well with hime that he semeth to be therunto given by nature."

Ellis, i. 343-4.

Of the course of study of ' well-bred youths' in the early years of Elizabeth's reign we have an interesting account by Sir Nicholas Bacon, Lord Keeper, father of the great Bacon, in a Paper by Mr J. Payne Collier in the *Archæologia*, vol. 36, Part 2, p. 339, Article xxxi.[2]   " Before he became Lord Keeper, Sir Nicholas Bacon had been Attorney of that Court" [the Court of Wards and Liveries] " a most lucrative appointment ; and on the 27th May, 1561, he addressed a letter to Sir William Cecil, then recently (Jan., 1561) made Master of the Wards, followed by a paper thus entitled :—' Articles devised for the bringing up in vertue and learning of the Queenes Majesties Wardes, being heires males, and whose landes, descending in pos-session and coming to the Queenes Majestie, shall amount to the cleere yearly value of c. markes, or above.'"   Sir Nicholas asks the new Master of Wards to reform what he justly calls most " prepos-terous" abuses in the department :—" That the proceeding hath bin preposterous, appeareth by this : the chiefe thinge, and most of price, in wardeship, is the wardes mynde ; the next to that, his bodie ; the

---

[1] Ascham praises most the practice of double translation, from Latin into English, and then back from English into Latin.—*Scholemaster*, p. 90, 178, ed. Giles.

[2] Mr Wm. Chappell gives me the reference, and part of the extract.

last and meanest, his land. Nowe, hitherto the chiefe care of govern-
aunce hath bin to the land, being the meaneste; and to the bodie,
being the better, very small; but to the mynde, being the best, none
at all, which methinkes is playnely to sett the carte before the horse"
(p. 343). Mr Collier then summarises Bacon's Articles for the
bringing up of the Wards thus: " The wards are to attend divine
service at six in the morning : nothing is said about breakfast,[1] but
they are to study Latin until eleven; to dine between 11 and 12 ; to
study with the music-master from 12 till 2; from 2 to 3 they are to
be with the French master; and from 3 to 5 with the Latin and
Greek masters. At 5 they are to go to evening prayers; then they
are to sup; to be allowed honest pastimes till 8 ; and, last of all,
before they go to bed at 9, they are again to apply themselves to
music under the instruction of the master. At and after the age of
16 they were to attend lectures upon temporal and civil law, as well
as *de disciplinâ militari*. It is not necessary to insert farther
details; but what I have stated will serve to show how well-bred
youths of that period were usually brought up, and how disgracefully
the duty of education as regards wards was neglected. . . It may
appear singular that in these articles drawn up by Sir Nicholas, so
much stress is laid upon instruction in music[2]; but it only serves to
confirm the notion that the science was then most industriously cul-
tivated by nearly every class of society." Pace in 1517 requires that
every one should study it, but should join with it some other study,
as Astrology or Astronomy. He says also that the greatest part of
the art had perished by men's negligence; "For all that our
musicians do now-a-days, is almost trivial if compared with what the
old ones (*antiqui*) did, so that now hardly one or two (*unus aut
alter*) can be found who know what harmony is, though the word is
always on their tongue." (*De Fructu*, p. 54-5.) Ascham, while
lamenting in 1545 (*Toxophilus*, p. 29) 'that the laudable custom of

[1] When did *breakfast* get its name, and its first notice as a regular meal? I
do not remember having seen the name in the early part of *Household Ordinances*,
or any other work earlier than the *Northumberland Household Book*.
[2] On Musical Education, see the early pages of Mr Chappell's *Popular Music*,
and the note in Archæol., vol. xx, p. 60-1, with its references. ' Music constituted
a part of the *quadrivium*, a branch of their system of education.'

England to teach children their plain song and prick-song' is 'so decayed throughout all the realm as it is,' denounces the great practise of instrumental music by older students : " the minstrelsy of lutes, pipes, harps, and all other that standeth by such nice, fine, minikin fingering, (such as the most part of scholars whom I know use, if they use any,) is far more fit, for the womanishness of it, to dwell in the Court among ladies, than for any great thing in it which should help good and sad study, to abide in the University among scholars."

By 1574 our rich people, according to Harrison, attended properly to the education of their children.   After speaking " of our women, whose beautie commonlie exceedeth the fairest of those of the maine," he says :

" This neuerthelesse I vtterlie mislike in the poorer sort of them, for the wealthier doo sildome offend herein : that being of themselues without competent wit, they are so carelesse in the education of their children (wherein their husbands also are to be blamed,) by means whereof verie manie of them neither fearing God, neither regarding either manners or obedience, do oftentimes come to confusion, which (if anie correction or discipline had beene vsed toward them in youth) might haue prooued good members of their common-wealth & countrie, by their good seruice and industrie."—*Descr. of Britaine*, Holinshed, i. 115, col. 2.

This is borne out by Ascham, who says that young men up to 17 were well looked after, but after that age were turned loose to get into all the mischief they liked :

" In deede, from seven to seventene, yong jentlemen commonlie be carefullie enough brought up : But from seventene to seven and twentie (the most dangerous tyme of all a mans life, and most slipperie to stay well in) they have commonlie the rein of all licens in their owne hand, and speciallie soch as do live in the Court.   And that which is most to be merveled at, commonlie the wisest and also best men be found the fondest fathers in this behalfe.   And if som good father wold seek some remedie herein, yet the mother (if the household of our Lady) had rather, yea, and will to, have her sonne cunnyng and bold, in making him to lyve trimlie when he is yong, than by learning and travell to be able to serve his Prince & his countrie, both wiselie in peace, and stoutlie in warre, whan he is old.

" The fault is in your selves, ye noble mens sonnes, and therfore ye deserve the greater blame, that commonlie the meaner mens children cum to be the wisest councellours, and greatest doers, in the weightie affaires of this realme."—*Scholemaster*, ed. Mayor, p. 39-40.

Note lastly, on this subject of private tuition, that Mulcaster in

his *Elementarie*, 1582, complains greatly of rich people aping the
custom of princes in having private tutors for their boys, and with-
drawing them from public schools where the spirit of emulation
against other boys would make them work.　The course he recom-
mends is, that rich people should send their sons, with their tutors,
to the public schools, and so get the advantage of both kinds of tuition.

　Girls' Home Education.　The earliest notice of an English
Governess that any friend has found for me is in "the 34th Letter
of Osbert de Clare in Stephen's reign, A.D. 1135-54.　He mentions
what seems to be a Governess of his children, '*quædam matrona quæ
liberos ejus* (sc. *militis, Herberti de Furcis*) *educare consueverat.*'　She
appears to be treated as one of the family : e. g. they wait for her
when she goes into a chapel to pray.　I think a nurse would have
been '*ancilla quæ liberos ejus nutriendos susceperat.*' "　Walter de
Biblesworth was the tutor of the "lady Dionysia de Monchensi, a
Kentish heiress, the daughter of William de Monchensi, baron of
Swanescombe, and related, apparently, to the Valences, earls of
Pembroke, and wrote his French Grammar, or rather Vocabulary[1],
for her.　She married Hugh de Vere, the second son of Robert,
fifth earl of Oxford. (Wright.)　Lady Jane Grey was taught
by a tutor at home, as we have seen.　Palsgrave was tutor to
Henry VIII.'s "most dere and most entirely beloved suster, quene
Mary, douagier of France," and no doubt wrote his *Lesclaircissement de
la Langue Francoise* mainly for her, though also "desirous to do
some humble service unto the nobilitie of this victorious realme, and
universally unto all other estates of this my natyfe country."　Giles
Du Guez, or as Palsgrave says to Henry VIII., "the synguler clerke,
maister Gyles Dewes, somtyme instructor to your noble grace in this
selfe tong, at the especiall instaunce and request of dyvers of your
highe estates and noble men, hath also for his partye written in this
matter."　His book is entitled "An Introductorie for to lerne to
rede, to pronounce & to speke French trewly : compyled for the
Right high, excellent, and most vertuous lady The Lady Mary of

---

[1] Le treytyz ke moun sire Gauter de Biblesworthe fist à MA DAME DYONISIE DE
MOUNCHENSY, pur aprise de langwage.

Englande, doughter to our most gracious soverayn Lorde Kyng Henry the Eight."

3. *English University Education.* In early days Cambridge and Oxford must be looked on, I suppose, as mainly the great schools for boys, and the generality of scholars as poor men's children,[1] like Chaucer's ' poore scolares tuo that dwelten in the soler-halle of Cantebregge,' his Clerk of Oxenford, and those students, gifts to whom are considered as one of the regular burdens on the husbandman, in "God speed the Plough." Mr Froude says, Hist. of England, I. 37 :

" The universities were well filled, by the sons of yeomen chiefly. The cost of supporting them at the colleges was little, and wealthy men took a pride in helping forward any boys of promise[2] (*Latimer's Sermons*, p. 64). It seems clear also, as the Reformation drew nearer, while the clergy were sinking lower and lower, a marked change for the better became perceptible in a portion at least of the laity."

But Grosseteste mentions a "noble" scholar at Oxford (*Epist.* 129), and Edward the Black Prince and Henry V. are said to have been students of Queen's College, Oxford. Wolsey himself was a College tutor at Oxford, and had among his pupils the sons of the Marquess of Dorset, who afterwards gave him his first preferment, the living of Lymington. (Chappell.)

[1] Later on, the proportions of poor and rich changed, as may be inferred from the extract from Harrison below. In the ' exact account of the whole number (2920) of Scholars and Students in the University of Oxford taken anno 1612 in the Long Vacation, the *Studentes* of Christ Church are 100, the *Pauperes Scholares et alii Servientes* 41; at Magdalene the latter are 76; at New College 18, to 70 *Socii ;* at Brasenose (*Æneasense* Coll.) the *Communarii* are 145, and the *Pauperes Scholares* 17; at Exeter, the latter are 37, to 134 *Communarii ;* at St John's, 20 to 43 ; at Lincoln the *Communarii* are 60, to 27 *Batellatores et Pauperes Scholares.*' Collectanea Curiosa, v. i. p. 196-203.

[2] Was this in return for the raised rents that Ascham so bitterly complains of the new possessors of the monastic lands screwing out of their tenants, and thereby ruining the yeomen ? He says to the Duke of Somerset on Nov. 21, 1547 (ed. Giles, i. p. 140-1),

Qui auctores sunt tantæ miseriæ ? . . Sunt illi qui hodie passim, in Anglia, prædia monasteriorum gravissimis annuis reditibus auxerunt. Hinc omnium rerum exauctum pretium; hi homines expilant totam rempublicam. Villici et coloni universi laborant, parcunt, corradunt, ut istis satisfaciant. . . Hinc tot familiæ dissipatæ, tot domus collapsæ . . Hinc, quod omnium miserrimum est, nobile illud decus et robur Angliæ, nomen, inquam, *Yomanorum Anglorum*, fractum et collisum est. . . NAM VITA, QUÆ NUNC VIVITUR A PLURIMIS, NON VITA, SED MISERIA EST.

When will these words cease to be true of our land ? They should be burnt into all our hearts.

The legend runs that the first school at Oxford was founded by King Alfred[1], and that Oxford was a place of study in the time of Edward the Confessor (1041-66). If one may quote a book now considered to be ' a monkish forgery and an exploded authority,' Ingulfus, who was Abbot of Croyland, in the Isle of Ely, under William the Conqueror, says of himself that he was educated first at Westminster, and then passed to Oxford, where he made proficiency in such books of Aristotle as were then accessible to students,[2] and in the first two books of Tully's Rhetoric.—*Malden*, On the Origin of Universities, 1835, p. 71.

In 1201 Oxford is called a *University*, and said to have contained 3000 scholars; in 1253 its first College (University) is founded. In 1244, Hen. III. grants it its first privileges as a corporate body, and confirms and extends them in 1245. In his reign, Wood says the number of scholars amounted to 30,000, a number no doubt greatly exaggerated.

In the reign of Stephen it is said that Vacarius, a Lombard by birth, who had studied the civil law at Bologna, came into England, and formed a school of law at Oxford[3] . . he remained in England in the reign of Henry II. On account of the difficulty and expense of obtaining copies of the original books of the Roman law, and *the poverty of his English scholars*, Vacarius [ab. 1149, A.D.] compiled an abridgment of the Digests and Codex, in which their most essential parts were preserved, with some difference of arrangement, and illustrated from other law-books. . . It bore on its title that it was "*pauperibus presertim destinatus ;*" and hence the Oxford students of law obtained the name of *Pauperists.*—*Malden*, p. 72-3.

Roger Bacon (who died 1248) speaks of a young fellow who came

---

[1] " He placed Æthelweard, his youngest son, who was fond of learning, together with the sons of his nobility, and of many persons of inferior rank, in schools which he had established with great wisdom and foresight, and provided with able masters. In these schools the youth were instructed in reading and writing both the Saxon and Latin languages, and in other liberal arts, before they arrived at sufficient strength of body for hunting, and other manly exercises becoming their rank." Henry, *History of England*, vol. ii. pp. 354-5 (quoted from Asser).

[2] None were so. T. Wright.

[3] Professor Rogers says : " There is *no* evidence that Vacarius lectured at Oxford. The statement is a mistake made by Hallam on a passage in John of Salisbury quoted by Selden."

to him, aged 15, not having wherewithal to live, or finding proper
masters : "because he was obliged to serve those who gave him
necessaries, during two years found no one to teach him a word in
the things he learned."—*Opus Tertium*, cap. xx. In 1214 the Commonalty of Oxford agreed to pay 52s. yearly for the use of poor
scholars, and to give 100 of them a meal of bread, ale, and pottage,
with one large dish of flesh or fish, every St Nicholas day.—*Wood's An.*
i. 185. *Wood's Annals* (ed. Gutch, v. i. p. 619-20) also notes that
in 1461 A.D. divers Scholars were forced to get a license under the
Chancellor's hand and seal (according to the Stat. 12 Ric. II., A.D.
1388, *Ib.*, p. 519) to beg : and Sir Thos. More says "then may wee
yet, like poor Scholars of Oxford, go a begging with our baggs &
wallets, & sing salve Regina at rich mens dores." On this point we
may also compare the Statutes of Walter de Merton for his College
at Oxford, A.D. 1274, ed. Halliwell, 1843, p. 19 :

Cap. 13. De admissione scholarium.

Hoc etiam in eadem domo specialiter observari volo et decerno, ut
circa eos, qui ad hujusmodi eleemosinæ participationem admittendi
fuerint, diligenti solicitudine caveatur, ne qui præter castos, honestos,
pacificos, humiles, *indigentes*, ad studium habiles ac proficere volentes,
admittantur. Ad quorum agnitionem singulis, cum in dicta societate
fuerint admittendi sustentationis gratia in eadem, ad annum unum
utpote probationis causa primitus concedatur, ut sic demum si in
dictis conditionibus laudabiliter se habuerint, in dictam congrega-
tionem admittantur.

See also cap. 31, against horses of scholars being kept.

Lodgings were let according to the joint valuation of 2 Magistri
(scholars) and two townsmen (probi et legales homines de Villa).
Wood, i. 255. An. 15 Hen. III. A.D. 1230-1.

In the beginning of the 15th century it had become the established rule that every scholar must be a member of some college or
hall. The scholars who attended the public lectures of the university, without entering themselves at any college or hall, were called
chamber dekyns, as in Paris they were called martinets ; and frequent enactments were made against them.—*Mullen*, p. 85, ref. to
Wood's Annals, 1408, -13, -22, and 1512, &c.

The following are the dates of the foundations of the different
Colleges at Oxford as given in the University Calendar :—

University College,	1253-80[1]	Magdalen	„	.. 1458
Balliol Coll., betw.	1263 & 1268	The King's Hall and College of Brasenose	}	1509
Merton College, founded at				
Maldon, in Surrey, in		Corpus Christi College	` ..	1516
1264, removed to Oxford		Christ Church	..	.. 1526
in	..	.. 1274	Trinity College	..	.. 1554
Exeter College	`..	.. 1314	St John's	„	.. 1555
Oriel	„	.. 1326	Jesus	„	.. 1571
The Queen's College		.. 1340	Wadham	„	.. 1613
New	„	.. 1386	Pembroke	„	.. 1624
Lincoln	„	.. 1427	Worcester	„	.. 1714
All Souls	„	.. 1437			

HALLS.

St Edmund Hall	..	.. 1317	Magdalen Hall	..	.. 1487
St Mary's	„	.. 1333	St Alban	„	.. after 1547
New Inn	„	.. 1438			

'The Paston Letters' do not give us much information about studies or life at Oxford, but they do give us material for estimating the cost of a student there (ii. 124[2]) ; they show us the tutor reporting to a mother her son's progress in learning (ii. 130), and note the custom of a man, when made bachelor, giving a feast : " I was made bachelor .. on Friday was se'nnight (18 June, 1479), and I made my feast on the Monday after (21 June). I was promised venison against my feast, of my Lady Harcourt, and of another person too, but I was deceived of both ; but my guests held them pleased with such meat as they had, blessed be God." The letter as to the costs is dated May 19, 1478.

" I marvel sore that you sent me no word of the letter which I sent to you by Master William Brown at Easter. I sent you word that time that I should send you mine expenses particularly ; but as at this time the bearer hereof had a letter suddenly that he should come home, & therefore I could have no leisure to send them to you on that wise, & therefore I shall write to you in this letter the whole sum of my expenses since I was with you till Easter last past, and

[1] This College is said to have been founded in the year 872, by Alfred the Great. It was restored by William of Durham, said to have been Archdeacon of Durham ; but respecting whom little authentic information has been preserved, except that he was Rector of Wearmouth in that county, and that he died in 1249, bequeathing a sum of money to provide a permanent endowment for the maintenance of a certain number of "Masters." The first purchase with this bequest was made in 1253, and the first Statutes are dated 1280.—*Oxford Univ. Calendar*, 1865, p. 167.

[2] I refer to the modernized edition published by Charles Knight in two volumes.

also the receipts, reckoning the twenty shillings that I had of you to
Oxon wards, with the bishop's finding :—

	£	s.	d.
The whole sum of receipts is	5	17	6
And the whole sum of expenses is	6	5	5¾
And that [=what] cometh over my receipts & my expenses I have borrowed of Master Edmund, & it draweth to		8	0

and yet I reckon none expenses since Easter; but as for them, they
be not great."

On this account Fenn says,

" he (Wm. Paston) had expended £6 5s. 5¾d. from the time he
left his mother to Easter last, which this year fell on the 22nd
March, from which time it was now two months, & of the expenses
' since incurred' he says 'they be not great.' We may therefore conclude the former account was from the Michaelmas preceding, and a
moderate one ; if so, we may fairly estimate his university education
at £100 a-year of our present money. I mean that £12 10s. 11½d.
would then procure as many necessaries and comforts as £100 will
at this day."

What was the basis of Fenn's calculation he does not say. In
1468, the estimates for the Duke of Clarence's household expenses
give these prices, among others :

	s.	d.		£	s.	d.
Wheat, a quarter	6	0	now, say	3	0	0
Ale, a gallon		1½	,,		1	0
Beves, less hide and tallow, each	10	0	,,	15	0	0*
Muttons ,, ,,	1	4	,,	2	10	0*
Velys ,, ,,	2	6	,,	4	0	0*
Porkes ,, ,,	2	0	,,	5	0	0
Rice, a pound		3	,,			5
Sugar ,,		6	,,			6
Holland, an ell (6d., 8d., 16d.)		10	,,		1	3
Diapre ,,	4	6	,,		3	0
Towelles ,,	1	8	,,		1	6
Napkyns, a dozen, 12s., £1, £2,	17	4	,,	2	0	0
	£2	7	0½		£31	17	8

This sum would make the things named nearly 14 times as dear
now as in 1468, and raise Fenn's £100 to about £180; but no
reliance can be placed on this estimate because we know nothing of
the condition of the beves, muttons, veles, and porkys, then, as con-

* Poor ones.

trasted with ours. Possibly they were half the size and half the weight. Still, I have referred the question to Professor Thorold Rogers, author of the *History of Prices* 1250-1400 A.D., and he says :

" In the year to which you refer (1478) bread was very dear, 50 per cent. above the average. But on the whole, wheat prices in the 15th century were lower than in the 14th. Fenn's calculation, a little below the mark for wheat, is still less below it in most of the second necessaries of life. The multiple of wheat is about 9, that of meat at least 24, those of butter and cheese nearly as much. But that of clothing is not more than 6, that of linen from 4 to 5. Taking however one thing with another, 12 is a safe general multiplier."

This would make the cost of young Paston's university education £150 11s. 6d. a year.

Mr Whiston would raise Fenn's estimate of £100 to £200. He says that the rent of land in Kent in 1540 was a shilling or eighteenpence an acre,—see *Valor Ecclesiasticus,*—and that the tithes and glebes of the Dean and Chapter of Rochester, which were worth about £480 a-year in 1542, are now worth £19,000.

The remaining Oxford letter in the Paston volumes seems to allude to the students bearing part of the expenses of the degree, or the feast at it, of a person related to royal family.

" I supposed, when that I sent my letter to my brother John, that the Queen's brother should have proceeded at Midsummer, and therefore I beseeched her to send me some money, *for it will be some cost to me,* but not much."

The first school at Cambridge is said to have been founded by Edward the Elder, the son of Alfred, but on no good authority. In 1223 the term *University* was applied to the place. The dates of the foundations of its Colleges, as given in its Calendar, are :

St Peter's	..	.. 1257	St Catherine's Hall	..	1473
(date of charter, 1264)			Jesus	..	.. 1496
Clare Hall..	..	.. 1326	Christ's	..	.. 1505
Pembroke ..	..	... 1347	St John's ..	..	.. 1511
Caius	..	.. 1349	Magdalene..	..	.. 1519
Trinity Hall	..	.. 1350	Trinity	..	.. 1546
Corpus Christi	..	.. 1351	Emmanuel..	..	.. 1584
King's	..	.. 1441	Sidney	..	.. 1598
Queen's	..	.. 1446	Downing ..	..	.. 1800
(refounded 1465)					

Lord Henry Brandon, son of the Duke of Suffolk, died of the

sweating sickness then prevalent in the University, on the 16th July, 1551, while a student of Cambridge. His brother, Lord Charles Brandon, died on the same day. Their removal to Buckden was too late to save them (*Ath. Cant.*, i. 105, 541). Of them Ascham says ' two noble Primeroses of Nobilitie, the yong Duke of Suffolke and Lord *H. Matrevers* were soch two examples to the Courte for learnyng, as our tyme may rather wishe, than look for agayne.'—*Scholemaster*, ed. Mayor, p. 62. Besides these two young noblemen, the first 104 pages of Cooper's *Athenæ Cantabrigienses* disclose only one other, Lord Derby's son, and the following names of sons of knights : [1]

CAMBRIDGE MEN.

1443 Thomas Rotherham, Fellow of King's, son of Sir Thomas Rotherham, knight, and Alice his wife.

1494 Reginald Bray, high-steward of the university of Oxford, son of Sir Richard Bray, knight, and the lady Joan his second wife.

---

[1] Other well-born men, in the *Ath. Cant.*, then connected with the University, or supposed to be, were,

1504 Sir Roger Ormston, knight, died. Had been High Steward of the University.

1504 Sir John Mordaunt, High Steward.

1478 George Fitzhugh, 4th son of Henry lord Fitzhugh, admitted B.A.

1488 Robert Leyburn, born of a knightly family, Fellow of Pembroke-hall, and proctor.

1457 John Argentine, of an ancient and knightly family, was elected from Eton to King's.

1504 Robert Fairfax, of an ancient family in Yorkshire, took the degree of Mus. Doc.

1496 Christopher Baynbrigg, of a good family at Hilton, near Appleby, educated at and Provost of Queen's, Oxford, incorporated of Cambridge.

1517 Sir Wm. Fyndern, knight, died, and was a benefactor to Clare Hall, in which it is supposed he had been educated.

1481 Robert Rede, of an ancient Northumbrian family, was sometime of Buckingham College, and the Fellow of King's-hall (?), and was autumn reader at Lincoln's Inn in 1481.

ab. 1460 Marmaduke Constable, son of Sir Robert Constable, knight, believed to have been educated at Cambridge.

,,   So, Edward Stafford, heir of Henry Stafford, Duke of Buckingham, is also believed to have been educated at Cambridge, because his father was a munificent patron of the University, constantly maintaining, or assisting to maintain, scholars therein.

,,   So, Thomas Howard, son of Sir John Howard, knight, and afterwards Duke of Norfolk, who defeated the Scots at Flodden, is believed, &c.

1484 John Skelton, the poet, probably of an ancient Cumberland family.

1520 ? Henry Howard, son of Lord Thomas Howard, ultimately Duke of Norfolk. Nothing is known as to the place of his education. If it were either of the English Universities, the presumption is in favour of Cambridge.

The only tradesman's son mentioned is,

1504 Sir Richard Empson, son of Peter Empson, a sieve-maker, High-Steward.

1502 Humphrey Fitzwilliam, of Pembroke Hall, Vice-Chancellor, *appears* to have been the son of Sir Richard Fitzwilliam of Ecclesfield, and Elizabeth his wife.

ab. 1468 Richard Redman, son of Sir Richard Redman and Elizabeth [Aldburgh] his wife; made Bp. of St Asaph.

1492 Thomas Savage, son of Sir John Savage, knight, Bp. of Rochester. Was LL.D. ? educated at Cambridge.

1485 James Stanley, younger son of Thomas Earl of Derby, . educated at both universities, graduated at Cambridge, and became prebendary of Holywell in 1485, Bp. of Ely in 1506.

1497 William Coningsby, son of Sir Humphrey Coningsby, elected from Eton to King's.

1507 Thomas Elyot, son of Sir Richard Elyot, made M.A.

ab. 1520 George Blagge, son of Sir Robert Blagge.

Queen Elizabeth's favourite, Lord Essex, was at Trinity College, Cambridge. See his letter of May 13, from there, in Ellis, series II. v. iii. p. 73; the furniture of his room, and his expenses, in the note p. 73-4; and his Tutor's letter asking for new clothes for 'my Lord,' or else 'he shall not onely be thrid bare, but ragged.'

Archbp. Whitgift[1], when B.D. at Pembroke Hall, Cambridge, A.D. 1563, "bestowed some of his time and abilities in the instruction of ingenious youth, sent to the college for education, in good learning and Christian manners. And among such his pupils, were two noblemen's sons, viz. the Lord Herbert, son and heir to the Earl of Pembroke; and John, son and heir to the Lord North." (*Life*, by Strype, ed. 1822, vol. i. p. 14.)

While Whitgift was Master of Trinity, Strype says he had bred up under him not only several Bishops, but also "the Earls of Worcester and Cumberland, the Lord Zouch, the Lord Dunboy of Ireland, Sir Nicolas and Sir Francis Bacon. To which I may add one more, namely, the son of Sir Nicolas White, Master of the Rolls in Ireland, who married a Devereux." (*Life*, i. 157, ed. 1822.)

A search through the whole of the first volume of Wood's *Athenæ Oxonienses*, comprising a period of nearly 100 years, has resulted in the following meagre list of men of noble or knightly birth who distinguished themselves. There are besides many men of "genteel

---

[1] Whitgift himself, born 1530, was educated at St Paul's school, then sent back to his father in the country, and sent up to Cambridge in 1548 or 1549.

parents," some of trader-ones, many friars, some Winchester men, but no Eton ones, educated at Oxford.

1478 Edmund Dudley, son of John Dudley, Esq., 2nd son of John Lord Dudley, of Dudley Castle in Staffordshire.

ab. 1483 John Colet, the eldest son of Sir Henry Colet, twice lord mayor of London . . was educated in grammaticals, partly in London or Westminster.

„ Nicholas Vaux, son of Sir Will. Vaux of Harwedon in Northamptonshire (not the Poet, Lord Vaux).

end of John Bourchier, Lord Berners, eldest son of Sir John Edw. IV. Bourchier, knight, Lord Berners of Hertfordshire . . was instructed in several sorts of learning in the university in the latter end of K. Edw. IV.; in whose reign, and before, were the sons of divers of the English nobility educated in academical literature in Baliol Coll.,[1] wherein, as 'tis probable, this our author was instructed also.

1497 Thomas More, son of Sir John More, knight. (*The* Sir Thomas More.)

? ab. 1510 George Bulleyn, son and heir of Sir Tho. Bullen, and sister of Anne Bulleyn.

? „ Henry Parker, son of Sir William Parker, knight.

1515 Christopher Seintgerman, son of Sir Henry Seintgerman, knight.

? ab. 1520 Thomas Wyatt, son of Henry Wyatt of Alington Castle in Kent, knight and baronet, migrated from St John's, Cambridge.[2]

1538 [3] John Heron, a Kentish man born, near of kin to Sir John Heron, knight.

? ab. 1520 Edward Seymoure, son of Sir John Seymoure, or St Maure of Wolf-hall in Wilts, knight, was educated in trivials, and partly in quadrivials for some time in this university. He was Jane Seymour's brother, and afterwards Duke of Somerset, and was beheaded on Jan. 22, 1552-3.

1534 John Philpot, son of Sir Pet. Philpot, knight of the Bath. Fellow of New Coll.

ab. 15— Henry Lord Stafford (author of the *Mirror for Magistrates*), the only son of Edward, Duke of Bucks, 'received

[1] No proof of this is given.

[2] Henry Howard, Earl of Surrey, son and heir of Thomas Duke of Norfolk, ' was for a time student in Cardinal Coll. as the constant tradition has been among us.' p. 153, col. 1.

[3] Andrew Borde, who writes himself *Andreas Perforatus*, was born, as it seems, at Pevensey, commonly called Pensey [now Pemsey], in Sussex, and not unlikely educated in Wykeham's school near to Winchester, brought up at Oxford (as he saith in his *Introduction to Knowledge*, cap. 35), p. 170, col. 2, and note.

his education in both the universities, especially in that of
Cambridge, to which his father had been a benefactor.'

1515 Reynold Pole (the Cardinal), a younger son of Sir Rich.
Pole.

? ab. 1530 Anthony Browne, son of Sir Weston Browne, of Abbes-
roding and of Langenhoo in Essex, knight.

ab. 1574 Patrick Plunket, baron of Dunsary in Ireland, son of Rob.
Plunket, baron of the same place.

ab. 1570 Philip Sidney (the poet), son of Sir Henry Sidney.

?   John Smythe, son of Sir Clem. Smythe.
(Peter Levens or Levins, our *Manipulus* or Rhyming-
Dictionary man, became a student in the university, an.
1552, was elected probationer-fellow of Mag. Coll. into
a Yorkshire place, 18 Jan. 1557, being then bach. of
arts, and on the 19th Jan., 1559 was admitted true and
perpetual fellow. In 1560 he left his fellowship. *Ath.
Ox.* p. 547, col. 2.)

? ab. 1570 Reynolde Scot, a younger son of Sir John Scot of Scots-
hall, near to Smeeth in Kent.

1590 Hayward Townshend, eldest son of Sir Henry Townshend,
knight.

ab. 1587 Francis Tresham (of Gunpowder Plot notoriety), son of Sir
Thomas Tresham, knight.

The number of friars and monks at the Universities before the
Reformation, and especially at Oxford, must have been large. Tanner
says,

In our universities . . . were taught divinity and canon law
(then, t. Hen. III., much in vogue), and the friers resorting thither
in great numbers and applying themselves closely to their studies,
outdid the monks in all fashionable knowlédge.   But the monks
quickly perceived it, and went also to the universities and studied
hard, that they might not be run down by the friers.[1]   And as the

---

[1] See Mat. Paris, p. 665, though he speaks there chiefly of monks * beyond sea.

* As appears from Wood's *Fasti Oxon.*
The following names of Oxford men educated at monkish or friars' schools, or
of their bodies, occur in the first volume of Wood's *Athenæ Oxon.*, ed. Bliss:

p.   6, col. 2.   William Beeth, educated among the Dominicans or Black Friers
from his youth, and afterwards their provincial master or chief
governor.

p.   7, col. 2.   Richard Bardney, a Benedictine of Lincolnshire.

p. 11, col. 2.   John Sowle, a Carme of London.

p. 14, col. 1.   William Galeon, an Austin friar of Lynn Regis.

p. 18, col. 2.   Henry Bradshaw, one of the Benedictine monks of St Werberg's,
Chester.

p. 19, col. 1.   John Harley, of the order of the Preaching or Dominican, commonly
called Black, Friars.

D 2

friers got houses in the universities, the monks also got colleges
founded and endowed there[1] for the education of their novices, where
they were for some years instructed in grammar, philosophy, and school
divinity, and then returning home, improved their knowledge by
their private studies, to the service of God and the credit of their
respective societies.   So that a little before the Reformation, the
greatest part of the procceders in divinity at Oxford were monks and
Regular canons.

By Harrison's time, A.D. 1577[2], rich men's sons had not only
pressed into the Universities, but were scrooging poor men's sons out
of the endowments meant only for the poor, learning the lessons that
Mr Whiston so well shows our Cathedral dignitaries have carried out

[1] It was customary then at Oxford for the Religious to have schools that bore
the name of their respective orders ; as the Augustine, Benedictine, Carmelite, and
Franciscan schools ; and there were schools also appropriated to the benefit of particular Religious houses, as the Dorchester and Eynsham schools, &c.   The monks
of Gloucester had Gloucester convent, and the novices of Pershore an apartment in
the same house.   So likewise the young monks of Canterbury, Westminster, Durham,
St Albans, &c.   Kennet's Paroch. Antiq., p. 214.   So also Leland saith, Itin. vol. vi.
p. 28, that at Stamford the names of Peterborough Hall, Semplingham, and Vauldey
yet remain, as places whither the Religious of those houses sent their scholars to
study.   Tanner, Notitia Monastica, Preface, p. xxvi. note w.

[2] The abuse was of far earlier date than this.   Compare Mr Halliwell's quotation
in his 'Merton Statutes,' from his edition of 'the Poems of John Awdelay, the
blind poet of Haghmon Monastery in the 14th century,'

> Now ʒif a pore mon set hys son to Oxford to scole,
> Bothe the fader and the moder hyndryd they schal be ;
> And ʒif ther fallo a benefyse, hit schal be ʒif a folc,
> To a clerke of a kechyn, ore into the chaunceré . . .
>   Clerkys that han cunyng,
>   . . thai mai get no vaunsyng
>   Without symony.

---

p. 54, col. 2. Thomas Spenser, a Carthusian at Henton in Somersetshire ; ' whence
for a time he receded to Oxford (as several of his order did) to improve himself, or to pass a course, in theology.'
p. 94, col. 2. John Kynton, a Minorite or Grey-friar.
p. 101, col. 1. John Rycks,   ,,   ,,
p. 107, col. 1. John Forest, a Franciscan of Greenwich.
p. 189, col. 1. John Griffen, a Cistercian.
p. 278, col. 2. Cardinal Pole, educated among the Carthusians, and Carmelites or
' White-fryers.'
p. 363, col. 2. William Barlowe, an Austin of St Osith in Essex.
p. 630, col. 2. Henry Walpoole and Richard Walpoole, Jesuits.
The 5th Lord Percy, he of the *Household Book,* in the year 1520 founded an annual
stipend of 10 marcs for 3 years, for a *Pedagogus sive Magister, docens ac legens
Grammaticam et Philosophiam canonicis et fratribus* of the monastery of Alnwick
(Warton, ii. 492).

with the stipends of their choristers, boys and men. "*Les gros poissons mangent les menus.* Pro. Poore men are (easily) supplanted by the rich, the weake by the strong, the meane by the mighty." [1] (Cotgrave, u. *manger.*) The law of "natural selection" prevails. Who shall say nay in a Christian land professing the principles of the great "Inventor of Philanthropy"? Whitgift for one, see his Life of Strype, Bk. I. chap. xiii. p. 148-50, ed. 1822. In 1589 an act 31 Eliz. c. 6, was passed to endeavour to prevent the abuse, but, like modern Election-bribery Acts with their abuse, did not do it.

"at this present, of one sort & other, there are about three thousand students nourished in them both (as by a late serveie it manifestlie appeared). They [the Colleges at our Universities] were created by their founders at the first, onelie for pore men's sons, whose parents were not able to bring them up unto learning : but now they have the least benefit of them, by reason the rich do so incroch upon them. And so farre hath this inconvenence spread itself, that it is in my time an hard matter for a pore man's child to come by a fellowship (though he be neuer so good a scholer & worthie of that roome.) Such packing also is used at elections, that not he which best deserveth, but he that hath most friends, though he be the worst scholer, is alwaies surest to speed ; which will turne in the end to the overthrow of learning. That some gentlemen also, whose friends have been in times past benefactors to certeine of those houses, doe intrude into the disposition of their estates, without all respect of order or statutes devised by the founders, onelie thereby to place whome they think good (and not without some hope of gaine) the case is too too evident, and their attempt would soone take place, if their superiors did not provide to bridle their indevors. In some grammar schooles likewise, which send scholers to these universities, it is lamentable to see what briberie is used ; for yer the scholer can be preferred, such briberye is made, that pore men's children are commonly shut out, and the richer sort received (who in times past thought it dishonour to live as it were upon almes) and yet being placed, most of them studie little other than histories, tables, dice & trifles, as men that make not the living by their studie the end of their purposes; which is a lamentable bearing. Besides this, being for the most part either gentlemen, or rich men's sonnes, they oft bring the universities into much slander. [2] For

---

[1] Compare Chaucer : 'wherfore, as seith Senek, ther is nothing more covenable to a man of heigh estate than debonairté and pité ; and therfore thise flies than men clepen bees, whan thay make here king, they chesen oon that hath no pricke wherwith he may stynge.'—*Persones Tale,* Poet. Works, ed. Morris, iii. 301.

[2] Ascham complains of the harm that rich men's sons did in his time at Cambridge. Writing to Archbp. Cranmer in 1545, he complains of two *gravissima im-*

standing upon their reputation and libertie, they ruffle and roist it
out, exceeding in apparell, and hanting riotous companie (which
draweth them from their bookes into an other trade). And for
excuse, when they are charged with breach of all good order, thinke
it sufficient to saie, that they be gentlemen, which grieveth manie
not a little. But to proceed with the rest.

"Everie one of these colleges haue in like manner their pro-
fessors or readers of the tongs and severall sciences, as they call
them, which dailie trade up the youth there abiding privatlie in their
halles, to the end they may be able afterwards (when their turne
commeth about, which is after twelve termes) to show themselves
abroad, by going from thence into the common schooles and publike
disputations (as it were *In aream*) there to trie their skilles, ånd
declare how they have profited since their coming thither.

"Moreover in the publike schooles of both the universities, there
are found at the prince's charge (and that verie largelie) five pro-
fessors & readers, that is to saie, of divinitie, of the civill law,
physicke, the Hebrew and the Greek tongues. And for the other
lectures, as of philosophie, logike, rhetorike and the quadriuials,
although the latter (I mean, arithmetike, musike, geometrie and
astronomie, and with them all skill in the perspectives are now
smallie regarded in either of them) the universities themselves do
allowe competent stipends to such as reade the same, whereby they
are sufficiently provided for, touching the maintenance of their
estates, and no less encouraged to be diligent in their functions."

On the introduction of the study of Greek into the Universities,
Dr S. Knight says in his *Life of Colet:*

"As for *Oxford*, its own *History* and *Antiquities* sufficiently confess, that nothing was known there but *Latin*, and that in the most

pedimenta to their course of study: (1.) that so few old men will stop up to encourage
study by their example; (2.) " quod illi fere omnes qui huc Cantabrigiam confluunt,
pueri sunt, divitumque filii, et hi etiam qui nunquam inducunt animum suum, ut
abundanti aliqua perfectaque eruditione perpoliantur, sed ut ad alia reipublicæ
munera obeunda levi aliqua et inchoata cognitione paratiores efficiantur. Et hic
singularis quædam injuria bifariam academiæ intentata est; vel quia hoc modo omnis
expletæ absolutæque doctrinæ spes longe ante messem, in ipsa quasi herbescenti
viriditate, præciditur; vel quia omnis pauperum inopumque expectatio, quorum
ætates omnes in literarum studio conteruntur, ab his fucis eorum sedes occupantibus,
exclusa illusaque præripitur. Ingenium, enim, doctrina, inopia judicium, nil quic-
quam domi valent, ubi gratia, favor, magnatum literæ, et aliæ persimiles extraordi-
nariæ illegitimæque rationes vim foris adferunt. Hinc quoque illud accedit
incommodum, quod quidam prudentes viri nimis ægre ferunt partem aliquam regiæ
pecuniæ in collegiorum socios inpartiri; quasi illi non maxime indigeant, aut quasi
ulla spes perfectæ eruditionis in ullis aliis residere potest, quam in his, qui in per-
petuo literarum studio perpetuum vitæ suæ tabernaculum collocarunt. Ed. Giles, i.
p. 69-70. See also p. 121-2.

depraved Style of the *School-men*. *Cornelius Vitellius*, an *Italian*, was the first who taught *Greek* in that University [1] ; and from him the famous *Grocyne* learned the first Elements thereof.

" In *Cambridge*, *Erasmus* was the first who taught the *Greek Grammar*. And so very low was the State of Learning in that University, that (as he tells a Friend) about the Year 1485, the Beginning of *Hen*. VII. Reign, there was nothing taught in that publick Seminary besides *Alexander's Parva Logicalia*, (as they called them) the old *Axioms* of *Aristotle*, and the *Questions* of John Scotus, till in Process of time *good Letters* were brought in, and some Knowledge of the *Mathematicks*; as also *Aristotle* in a new Dress, and some Skill in the *Greek* Tongue ; and, by Degrees, a Multitude of *Authors*, whose *Names* before had not been heard of.[2]

" It is certain that even *Erasmus* himself did little understand *Greek*, when he came first into *England*, in 1497 (13 *Hen*. VII.), and that our Countryman *Linacer* taught it him, being just returned from *Italy* with great Skill in that Language : Which *Linacer* and *William Grocyne* were the two only Tutors that were able to teach it." Saml. Knight, Life of Dr John Colet, pp. 17, 18.

The age at which boys went up to the University seems to have varied greatly. When Oxford students were forbidden to play marbles they could not have been very old. But in "The Mirror of the Periods of Man's Life" (? ab. 1430 A.D.), in the Society's *Hymns to the Virgin and Christ* of this year, we find the going-up age put at twenty.

Quod resou*n*, in age of .xx. ʒeer,
Goo to oxenford, or lerne lawe[3].

This is confirmed by young Paston's being at Eton at nineteen (see below, p. lvi). In 1612, Brinsley (*Grammar Schoole*, p. 307) puts the age at fifteen, and says,

" such onely should be sent to the Vniuersities, who proue most ingenuous and towardly, and who, in a loue of learning, will begin to

---

[1] *Antea enim* Cornelius Vitellius, *homo* Italus Corneli, *quod est maritimum* Hetruriæ *Oppidum, natus nobili Prosapia, vir optimus gratiosusque, omnium primus* Oxonii *bonas literas docuerat*. [Pol. Verg. *lib.* xxvi.]

[2] *Ante annos ferme triginta, nihil tradebatur in schola* Cantabrigiensi, *præter* Alexandri Parva Logicalia, *ut vocant, & vetera illa* Aristotelis *dictata, Scoticasque Quæstiones. Progressu temporis accesserunt bonæ literæ ; accessit Matheseos Cognitio ; accessit novus, aut certe novatus,* Aristoteles ; *accessit* Græcarum *literarum peritia ; accesserunt Autores tam multi, quorum olim ne nomina quidem tenebantur*, &c. [Erasmi *Epist.* Henrico Bovillo, *Dat.* Roffæ *Cal.* Sept. 1516.]

[3] Sir John Fortescue's description of the study of law at Westminster and in the Inns of Chancery is in chapters 48-9 of his *De laudibus legum Angliæ*.

take paines of themselues, hauing attained in some sòrt the former parts of learning ; being good Grammarians at least, able to vnder-stand, write and speake Latine in good sort.

" Such as haue good discretion how to gouerne themselues there, and to moderate their expenses ; which is seldome times before 15 yeeres of age ; which is also the youngest age admitted by the statutes of the Vniuersity, as I take it."

4. Foreign University Education.

That some of our nobles sent their sons to be educated in the French universities (whence they sometimes imported foreign vices into England[1]) is witnessed by some verses in a Latin Poem " in MS. Digby, No. 4 (Bodleian Library) of the end of the 13th or beginning of the 14th century," printed by Mr Thomas Wright in his *Anecdota Literaria*, p. 38.

> Filii nobilium, dum sunt juniores,
> Mittuntur in Franciam fieri doctores ;
> Quos prece vel pretio domant corruptores,
> Sic prætaxatos referunt artaxata mores.

An English *nation* or set of students of the Faculty of Arts at Paris existed in 1169 ; after 1430 the name was changed to the German nation. Besides the students from the French provinces subject to the English, as Poictou, Guienne, &c., it included the English, Scottish, Irish, Poles, Germans, &c.—*Encyc. Brit.* John of Salisbury (born 1110) says that he was twelve years studying at Paris on his own account. Thomas a Becket, as a young man, studied at Paris. Giraldus Cambrensis (born 1147) went to Paris for edu-cation ; so did Alexander Neckham (died 1227). Henry says,

" The English, in particular, were so numerous, that they occupied several schools or colleges ; and made so distinguished a figure by their genius and learning, as well as by their generous manner of living, that they attracted the notice of all strangers. This appears from the following verses, describing the behaviour of a stranger on

---

[1] Mores habent barbarus, Latinus et Græcus ;
Si sacerdos, ut plebs est, cæcum ducit cæcus :
Se mares effeminant, et equa fit equus,
Expectes ab homine usque ad pecus.

Et quia non metuunt animæ discrimen,
Principes in habitum verterunt hoc crimen,
Varium viro turpiter jungit novus hymen,
Exagitata procul non intrat fœmina limen.

his first arrival in Paris, composed by Negel Wircker, an English student there, A.D. 1170 :—

> The stranger dress'd, the city first surveys,
> A church he enters, to his God he prays.
> Next to the schools he hastens, each he views,
> With care examines, anxious which to chuse.
> The English most attract his prying eyes,
> Their manners, words, and looks, pronounce them wise.
> Theirs is the open hand, the bounteous mind ;
> Theirs solid sense, with sparkling wit combin'd.
> Their graver studies jovial banquets crown,
> Their rankling cares in flowing bowls they drown.[1]

Montpelier was another University whither Englishmen resorted, and is to be remembered by us if only for the memory of Andrew Borde, M.D., some bits of whose quaintness are in the notes to Russell in the present volume.

Padua is to be noted for Pace's sake. He is supposed to have been born in 1482.

Later, the custom of sending young noblemen and gentlemen to Italy—to travel, not to take a degree—was introduced, and Ascham's condemnation of it, when no tutor accompanied the youths, is too well known to need quoting. The Italians' saying, *Inglese Italianato è un diabolo incarnato*, sums it up.[2]

5. *Monastic and Cathedral Schools.*

Herbert Losing, Bp. of Thetford, afterwards Norwich, between 1091 and 1119, in his 37th Letter restores his schools at Thetford to Dean Bund, and directs that no other schools be opened there.

Tanner (*Not. Mon.* p. xx. ed. Nasmith), when mentioning "the use and advantage of these Religious houses"—under which term

---

[1] Pixus et ablutus tandem progressus in urbem,
Intrat in ecclesiam, vota precesque facit.
Inde scholas adiens, secum deliberat, utrum
Expediat potius illa vel ista schola.
Et quia subtiles sensu considerat Anglos,
Pluribus ex causis se sociavit iis.
Moribus egregii, verbo vultuque venusti,
Ingenio pollent, consilioque vigent.
Dona pluunt populis, et detestantur avaros,
Fercula multiplicant, et sine lege bibunt.
A. Wood, *Antiq. Oxon.*, p. 55, in Henry's Hist. of Eng., vol. iii. p. 440-1.

[2] That Colet used his travels abroad, A.D. 1493-7, for a different purpose, see his Life by Dr Knight, pp. 23-4.

"are comprehended, cathedral and collegiate churches, abbies, priories, colleges, hospitals, preceptories (Knights Templars' houses), and frieries"— says,

"Secondly, They were schools of learning & education ; for every convent had one person or more appointed for this purpose ; and all the neighbours that desired it, might have their children taught grammar and church musick without any expence to them.[1]

In the nunneries also young women were taught to work, and to read English, and sometimes Latin also. So that not only the lower rank of people, who could not pay for their learning, but most of the noblemen and gentlemen's daughters were educated in those places."[2]

[1] Fuller, book vi. p. 297. Collier, vol. ii. p. 165. Stillingfleet's Orig. Britan. p. 206. Bishop Lloyd of Church Government, p. 160. This was provided for as early as A.D. 747, by the seventh canon of council of Clovesho, as Wilkins's Councils, vol. i. p. 95. See also the notes upon that canon, in Johnson's Collection of canons, &c. In Tavistock abbey there was a Saxon school, as Willis, i. 171. Tanner. (Charlemagne in his Capitularies ordained that each Monastery should maintain a School, where should be taught ' la grammaire, le calcule, et la musique.' See Démogeot's *Histoire de la Littérature Française*, p. 44, ed. Hachette. R. Whiston.) Henry says "these teachers of the cathedral schools were called *The scholastics* of the diocess ; and all the youth in it who were designed for the church, were intitled to the benefit of their instructions.* Thus, for example, William de Monte, who had been a professor at Paris, and taught theology with so much reputation in the reign of Henry II., at Lincoln, was the scholastic of that cathedral. By the eighteenth canon of the third general council of Lateran, A.D. 1179, it was decreed, That such scholastics should be settled in all cathedrals, with sufficient revenues for their support ; and that they should have authority to superintend all the schoolmasters of the diocess, and grant them licences, without which none should presume to teach. The laborious authors of the literary history of France have collected a very distinct account of the scholastics who presided in the principal cathedral-schools of that kingdom in the twelfth century, among whom we meet with many of the most illustrious names for learning of that age. . . . . . The sciences that were taught in these cathedral schools were such as were most necessary to qualify their pupils for performing the duties of the sacerdotal office, as Grammar, Rhetoric, Logic, Theology, and Church-Music."—*Ibid.* p. 442.

[2] Fuller and Collier, as before ; Bishop Burnet (Reform. vol. i. p. . .) saith so of Godstow. Archbishop Greenfield ordered that young gentlewomen who came to the nunneries either for piety or breeding, should wear white veils, to distinguish them from the professed, who wore black ones, 11 Kal. Jul. anno pontif. 6. M. Hutton. ex registr. ejus, p. 207. In the accounts of the cellaress of Carhow, near Norwich, there is an account of what was received " pro prebendationibus," or the board of young ladies and their servants for education "rec. de domina Margeria Wederly prehendinat, ibidem xi. septimanas xiii *s.* iv *d.* . . pro mensa unius famulæ dictæ Margeriæ per iii. septimanas viii *d.* per sept." &c. Tanner.

---

* Du Cange, Gloss. voc. *Scholasticus.*

As Lydgate (born at Lydgate in Suffolk, six or seven miles from
Newmarket) was ordained subdeacon in the Benedictine monastery
of Bury St Edmunds in 1389[1], he was probably sent as a boy to a
monastic school.   At any rate, as he sketches his early escapades—
apple-stealing, playing truant, &c.,—for us in his *Testament*[2], I shall
quote the youth's bit of the poem here :—

Harleian MS. 2255, fol. 60.

Duryng the tyme / of this sesoun ver   *In my boyhood,*
I meene the sesoun / of my yeerys greene
Gynnyng fro childhood / strecchithe[3] vp so fer
to þe yeerys / accountyd ful Fifteene   *up to 15,*
bexperience / as it was weel seene
The gerisshe sesoun / straunge of condiciouns
Dispoosyd to many vnbridlyd passiouns

[fol. 60 b.] ¶ Voyd of resoun / yove to wilfulnesse
Froward to vertu / of thrift gaf[4] litil heede
loth to lerne / lovid no besynesse   *I loved no work*
Sauf pley or merthe / straunge to spelle or reede   *but play,*
Folwyng al appetites / longyng to childheede
lihtly tournyng wylde / and seelde sad
Weepyng for nouht / and anoon afftir glad

¶ For litil wroth / to stryve with my felawe
As my passiouns / did my bridil leede
Of the yeerde somtyme / I Stood in awe   *yet I was afraid*
to be scooryd[5] / that was al my dreede   *of being scored by*
loth toward scole / lost my tyme in deede   *the rod.*
lik a yong colt / that ran with-owte brydil
Made my freendys / ther good to spend in ydil /

¶ I hadde in custom / to come to scole late   *I came to school*
Nat for to lerne / but for a contenaunce   *late,*
with my felawys / reedy to debate
to Iangle and Iape / was set al my plesaunce   *talked,*
wherof rebukyd / this was my chevisaunce
to forge a lesyng / and therupon to muse   *lied to get off*
whan I trespasyd / my silven to excuse   *blame,*

[fol. 61.] ¶ To my bettre / did no reverence   *and mocked my*
Of my sovereyns / gaf no fors at al   *masters.*

[1] Morley's *English Writers*, vol. ii. Pt. I. p. 421.
[2] Edited by Mr Halliwell in his 'Selection from the Minor Poems of Dan John Lydgate.' Percy Society, 1840, quoted by Prof. Morley.
[3] strecched. (These collations are from Harl. 218, fol. 65, back.)
[4] toke.   [5] skoured.

wex obstynat / by inobedience

I stole apples and grapes,

Ran in to garydns / applys ther I stal
To gadre frutys / sparyd hegg[1] nor wal
to plukke grapys / in othir mennys vynes
Was moor reedy / than for to seyn[2] matynes

played tricks and mocked people,

¶ My lust was al / to scorne folk and iape
Shrewde tornys / evir among to vse
to Skoffe and mowe[3] / lyk a wantoun Ape
whan I did evil / othre I did[4] accuse

liked counting cherry-stones better than church.

My wittys five / in wast I did abuse[5]
Rediere chirstoonys / for to[6] telle
Than gon to chirche / or heere the sacry[7] belle

Late to rise, I was ; dirty at dinner,

¶ Loth to ryse / lother to bedde at eve
with vnwassh handys[8] / reedy to dyneer
My *pater noster* / my *Crede* / or my beleeve
Cast at the[9] Cok / loo this was my maneer
Wavid with eche wynd / as doth a reed speer

deaf to the snub-bings of my friends,

Snybbyd[10] of my frendys / such techchys forta-mende[11]
Made deff ere / lyst nat / to them attende

[fol. 61 b.]

reckless in God's service,

¶ A child resemblyng / which was nat lyk to thryve
Froward to god / reklees[12] in his servise
loth to correccioun / slouhe my sylf to shryve
Al good thewys / reedy to despise

chief shammer of illness when I was well,

Cheef bellewedir / of feyned[13] trwaundise
this is to meene / my silf I cowde feyne
Syk lyk a trwaunt / felte[14] no maneer peyne

always unsteady,

¶ My poort my pas / my foot alwey vnstable
my look my eyen / vnswre and vagabounde
In al my werkys / sodeynly chaungable

ill-conducted,

To al good thewys / contrary I was founde
Now ovir sad / now moornyng / now iocounde

sparing none for my pleasure.

Wilful rekles / mad[15] stertyng as an hare
To folwe my lust / for no man wold I spare.

At these monastic schools, I suppose, were educated mainly
the boys whom the monks hoped would become monks, cleric or
secular ; mostly the poor, the Plowman's brother who was to be the
Parson, not often the ploughman himself. Once, though, made a
scholar and monk there, and sent by the Monastery to the University,
the workman's, if not the ploughman's, son, might rule nobles and

[1] nedir hegge.   [2] sey.   [3] mowen.   [4] koude.
[5] alle vse.   [6] cheristones to.   [7] sacryng.   [8] hondes.
[9] atte.   [10] Snybbyng.   [11] tumende.   [12] rekkes.
[13] froward.   [14] and felt.   [15] made.

sit by kings, nay, beard them to their face. Thomas a Becket, himself the son of poor parents, was sent to be brought up in the "religious house of the Canons of Merton."

In 1392 the writer of Piers Plowman's Crede sketches the then state of things thus :

Now mot ich soutere hys sone · seten to schole,
And ich a beggeres brol · on the book lerne,
And worth to a writere · and with a lorde dwelle,
Other falsly to a frere · the fend for to serven ;
So of that beggares brol · a [bychop[1]] shal worthen,
Among the peres of the lond · prese to sytten,
And lordes sones [2] lowly · to tho losels alowte,
Knyghtes crouketh hem to · and cruccheth ful lowe ;
And his syre a soutere · y-suled in grees,
His teeth with toylyng of lether · tatered as a sawe.

Side notes:
Now every cobbler's son and beggar's brat turns writer, then Bishop,

and lords' sons crouch to him,

a cobbler's son !

Here I might stop the quotation, but I go on, for justice has never yet been done [3] to this noble *Crede* and William's *Vision* as pictures of the life of their times,—chiefly from the profound ignorance of us English of our own language; partly from the grace, the freshness, and the brilliance of Chaucer's easier and inimitable verse :—

Alaas ! that lordes of the londe · leveth·swiche wrecchen,
And leveth swych lorels · for her lowe wordes.
They shulden maken [bichopes[1]] · her owen bretheren
        childre,
Other of som gentil blod · And so yt best semed,
And fostre none faytoures[1] · ne swich false freres,
To maken fat and fulle · and her flesh combren.
For her kynde were more · to y-clense diches
Than ben to sopers y-set first · and served with sylver.
A grete bolle-ful of benen · were beter in hys wombe,
And with the bandes[4] of bakun · his baly for to fillen
Than pertryches or plovers · or pecockes y-rosted,
And comeren her stomakes · with curiuse drynkes
That maketh swyche harlotes · hordom usen,
And with her wikkid word · wymmen bitrayeth.
God wold her wonyynge · were in wildernesse,
And fals freres forboden · the fayre ladis chaumbres ;
For knewe lordes her craft · treuly I trowe
They shulden nought haunten her house · so ho[m]ly[1]
        on nyghtes,

Side notes:
Lords

should make gentlemen Bishops,

and set these scamps

to clean ditches,

and eat beans and bacon-rind instead of peacocks,

and having women.

If Lords but knew their tricks,

[1] Mr Skeat's readings. The *abbot* and *abbots* of Mr Wright's text spoil the alliteration.

[2] Compare the previous passages under heading 1, p. vi.

[3] May Mr Skeat bring the day when it will be!   [4] ? randes. Sk.

they'd turn these beggars into the straw. Ne bedden swich brothels · in so brode shetes,
But sheten her heved in the stre · to sharpen her wittes.

There is one side of the picture, the workman's son turned monk, and clerk to a lord. Let us turn to the other side, the ploughman's son who didn't turn monk, whose head *was* 'shet' in the straw, who delved and ditched, and dunged the earth, eat bread of corn and bran, worts fleshless (vegetables, but no meat), drank water, and went miserably (*Crede*, l. 1565-71). What education did he get? To whom could he be apprenticed? What was his chance in life? Let the Statute-Book answer:—

A.D. 1388. 12º Rich. II., Cap. v.

Item. It is ordained & assented, That he or she which used to labour at the Plough and Cart, or other Labour or Service of Husbandry *till they be of the Age of Twelve Years, that from thenceforth they shall abide at the same Labour*, without being put to any Mystery or Handicraft; and if any Covenant or Bond of Apprentie (so) be from henceforth made to the Contrary, the same shall be holden for none.

A.D. 1405-6. 7º Henri IV., Cap. xvii.

. . . . . And Whereas in the Statutes made at Canterbury among other Articles it is contained That he or she that useth to labour at the Plough or Cart, or other Labour or Service of Husbandry, till he be of the age of Twelve Years, that from the same time forth he shall abide at the same Labour, without being put to any Mystery or Handicraft; and if any Covenant or Bond be made from that time forth to the contrary, it shall be holden for none: Notwithstanding which Article, and the good Statutes afore made through all parts of the Realm, the Infants born within the Towns and Seignories of Upland, whose Fathers & Mothers have no Land nor Rent nor other Living, but only their Service or Mystery, be put by their said Fathers and Mothers and other their Friends to serve, and bound Apprentices, to divers Crafts within the Cities and Boroughs of the said Realm *sometime at the Age of Twelve Years, sometime within the said Age*, and that for the Pride of Clothing and other evil Customs that Servants do use in the same; so that there is so great Scarcity of Labourers and other Servants of Husbandry *that the Gentlemen and other People of the Realm be greatly impoverished for the Cause aforesaid :* Our Sovereign Lord the King considering the said Mischief, and willing thereupon to provide Remedy, by the advice & assent of the Lords Spiritual and Temporal, and at the request of the said Commons, hath ordained and stablished, That no Man nor Woman, of what Estate or Condition they be, shall put their Son or Daughter, of whatsoever Age he or she be, to Serve as Apprentice to no Craft nor other Labour within any City or Borough in the Realm, except he have Land or Rent to the Value of Twenty Shillings by the Year at

the least, but they shall be put to other labours as their Estates doth
require, upon Pain of one Year's Imprisonment, and to make Fine and
Ransom at the King's Will.   And if any Covenant be made of any
such Infant, of what Estate that he be, to the contrary, it shall be
holden for none. Provided Always, that every Man and Woman, of
what Estate or Condition that he be, shall be free to set their Son or
Daughter to take Learning at any manner School that pleaseth them
within the Realm.

A most gracious saving clause truly, for those children who were used
to labour at the plough and cart till they were twelve years old.[1] Let
us hope that some got the benefit of it !

These Acts I came across when hunting for the Statutes
referred to by the *Boke of Curtasye* as fixing the hire of horses
for carriage at fourpence a piece, and they caused me some sur-
prise.   They made me wonder less at the energy with which
some people now are striving to erect " barriers against democracy"
to prevent the return match for the old game coming off.—However improving, and however justly retributive, future legislation
for the rich by the poor in the spirit of past legislation for the poor
by the rich might be, it could hardly be considered pleasant, and is
surely worth putting up the true barrier against, one of education in
each poor man's mind.   (He who americanizes us thus far will be the
greatest benefactor England has had for some ages.)—These Statutes
also made me think how the old spirit still lingers in England, how a
friend of my own was curate in a Surrey village where the kind-
hearted squire would allow none of the R's but Reading to be taught
in his school ; how another clergyman lately reported his Farmers'
meeting on the school question : Reading and Writing might be
taught, but Arithmetic not ; the boys would be getting to know too

[1] Later on, men's games were settled for them as well as their trades. In
A.D. 1541, the 33 Hen. VIII., cap. 9, § xvi., says,

" Be it also enacted by the authority aforesaid, That no manner of Artificer or
Craftsman of any Handicraft or Occupation, Husbandman, Apprentice, Labourer,
Servant at Husbandry, Journeyman or Servant of Artificer, Mariners, Fishermen,
Watermen or any Serving man, shall from the said feast of the Nativity of St John
Baptist play at the Tables, Tennis, Dice, Cards, Bowls, Clash, Coyting, Logating,
or any other unlawful Game out of Christmas, under the Pain of xx s. to be forfeit
for every Time ; (2) and in Christmas to play at any of the said Games in their
Master's Houses, or in their Master's Presence ; (3) and also that no manner of
persons shall at any time play at any Bowl or Bowls in open places out of his
Garden or Orchard, upon the Pain for every Time so offending to forfeit vi s. viiii d."
(For *Logating*, &c., see Strutt.)

much about wages, and that would be troublesome; how, lastly, our
gangs of children working on our Eastern-counties farms, and our
bird-keeping boys of the whole South, can almost match the children
of the agricultural labourer of 1388.'

The early practice of the Freemasons, and other crafts, refusing to
let any member take a bondsman's son as an apprentice, was founded
on the reasonable apprehension that his lord would or might afterwards claim the lad, make him disclose the trade-secrets, and carry on
his art for the lord's benefit. The fourth of the 'Fyftene artyculus
or fyftene poyntus' of the Freemasons, printed by Mr Halliwell
(p. 16), is on this subject.

Articulus quartus (MS. Bibl. Reg. 17 A, Art. I., fol. 3, &c.)

> The fowrthe artycul thys moste be,
> That the mayster hym wel be-se
> That he *no bondemon* prentys make,
> Ny for no covetyse do hym take;
> For the lord that he ys bond to,
> May fache the prentes whersever he go.
> 3ef yn the logge he were y-take,
> Muche desese hyt my3th ther make,
> And suche case hyt my3th befalle
> That hyt my3th greve summe or alle;
> For alle the masonus that ben there
> Wol stonde togedur hol y-fere.
> 3ef suche won yn that craft schulde dwelle,
> Of dyvers desesys 3e my3th telle.
> For more 3ese thenne, and of honesté,
> Take a prentes of herre [1] degré.
> By olde tyme, wryten y fynde
> That the prentes schulde be of gentyl kynde;
> And so sumtyme grete lordys blod
> Toke thys gemetry that ys ful good.

I should like to see the evidence of a lord's son having become a
working mason, and dwelling seven years with his master ' hys craft
to lurne.'

Cathedral Schools. About the pre-Reformation Schools I can
find only the extract from Tanner given above, p. xlii. On the post-
Reformation Schools I refer readers to Mr Whiston's *Cathedral
Trusts,* 1850. He says:

---

[1] higher.

"The Cathedrals of England are of two kinds, those of the old and those of the new foundation : of the latter, Canterbury (the old archiepiscopal see) and Carlisle, Durham, Ely, Norwich, Rochester, and Worcester, old episcopal sees, were A.D. 1541-2 refounded, or rather reformed, by Henry VIII. . . Besides these, he created five other cathedral churches or colleges, in connexion with the five new episcopal sees of Bristol, Chester, Gloucester, Oxford, and Peterborough. He further created the see of Westminster, which was . . subsequently (A.D. 1560) converted to a deanery collegiate by Queen Elizabeth. . . (p. 6). The preamble of the Act 31 Henry VIII. c. 9, for founding the new cathedrals, preserved in Henry's own handwriting, recites that they were established 'To the intente that Gods worde myght the better be sett forthe, *cyldren broght up in lernynge*, *clerces nuryshyd in the universities*, olde servantes decayed, to have lyfing, allmes housys for pour folke to be sustayned in, *Reders of grece, ebrew, and latyne to have good stypende*, dayly almes to be mynistrate, mending of hyght wayes, and exhybision for mynisters of the chyrche.' "

"A general idea of the scope and nature of the cathedral establishments, as originally planned and settled by Henry VIII., may be formed from the first chapter of the old statutes of Canterbury, which is almost identical with the corresponding chapter of the statutes of all the other cathedrals of the new foundation. It is as follows :

"On [1] the entire number of those who have their sustentation (qui sustentantur) in the cathedral and metropolitical church of Canterbury :

"First of all we ordain and direct that there be for ever in our aforesaid church, one dean, twelve canons, six preachers, twelve minor canons, one deacon, one subdeacon, twelve lay-clerks, *one master of the choristers, ten choristers, two teachers of the boys in grammar, one of whom is to be the head master, the other, second master, fifty boys to be instructed in grammar*,[2] twelve poor men to be maintained at the costs and charges of the said church, two vergers, two subsacrists (*i.e.*, sextons), four servants in the church to ring the bells, and arrange all the rest, two porters, who shall also be barber-tonsors, one caterer,[3] one butler, and one under butler, one cook, and one under-cook, who, indeed, in the number prescribed, are to serve in our church every one of them in his own order, according to our statutes and ordinances."

---

[1] Translated from the Latin copy in the British Museum, MS. Harl. 1197, art. 15, folio 319 b.

[2] Duodecim pauperes de sumptibus dictæ Ecclesiæ *alendi*.

[3] Duo *unus* Pincernæ, et *unus subpincerna*, duo unus cociquus, et unus subcoquus. Sic in MS.

E

In the Durham statutes, as settled in the first year of Philip and Mary, the corresponding chapter is as follows:

On [1] the total number of those who have their sustentation (qui sustentantur) in the cathedral church of Durham.

"We direct and ordain that there be for ever in the said church, one dean, twelve prebendaries, twelve minor canons, one deacon, one sub-deacon, ten clerks, (who may be either clerks or laymen,) *one master of the choristers, ten choristers, two teachers of the boys in grammar, eighteen boys to be instructed in grammar,* eight poor men to be maintained at the costs of the said church, two subsacrists, two vergers, two porters, one of whom shall also be barber-tonsor, one butler, one under-butler, one cook, and one under-cook."

"The monastic or collegiate character of the bodies thus constituted, is indicated by the names and offices of the inferior ministers above specified, who were intended to form a part of the establishment of the Common Hall, in which most of the subordinate members, including the boys to be instructed in grammar, were to take their meals. There was also another point in which the cathedrals were meant to resemble and supply the place of the old religious houses, *i. e.,* in the maintenance of a certain number of students at the universities."

R*t*. WHISTON, *Cathedral Trusts and their Fulfilment,* p. 2—4.

"The nature of these schools, and the desire to perpetuate and improve them, may be inferred from ' certein articles noted for the reformation of the cathedral churche of Excestr', submitted by the commissioners of Henry VIII., unto the correction of the Kynges Majestie,' as follows:

The tenth Article submitted. "That ther may be in the said Cathedral churche a free songe scole, the scolemaster to have yerly of the said pastor and prechars xx. marks for his wages, and his howss free, to teache xl. children frely, to rede, to write, synge and playe upon instruments of musike, also to teache ther A. B. C. in greke and hebrew. And every of the said xl. children to have wekely, xiid. for ther meat and drink, and yerly vi^s viii^d. for a gowne; they to be bownd dayly to syng *and* rede within the said Cathedral churche such divine service as it may please the Kynges Majestie to allowe; the said childre to be at comons alltogether, with three prests hereaffter to be spoke off, to see them well ordered at the meat and to reforme their manners."

Article the eleventh, submitted. "That ther may be a fre grammer scole within the same Cathedral churche, the scole-master to have xx^{li}. by yere and his howss fre, the ussher x^{li}. & his howss

---

[1] MS. No. 688 in Lambeth Library. MS. Harl. cod. 1594, art. 38, in Brit. Mus.

fre, and that the said pastor and prechars may be bound to fynd xl. children at the said grammer scole, giving to every oon of the children xiid. wekely, to go to commons within the citie at the pleasour of the frendes, so long to continew as the scolemaster do se them diligent to lerne. The pastor to appointe viii. every prechar iiii.· and the scolemaster iiii. ; the said childre serving in the said churche and going to scole, to be preferred before strangers ; provided always, that no childe be admitted to thexhibicion of the said churche, whose father is knowne to be worthe in goodes above ccc^li., or elles may dispend above xl^li. yerly enheritance."—*Ibid.*, p. 10—12.

" Now £300 at that time was worth about £5,000 now, so that these schools were *designed* for the lower ranks of society, and open to the sons of the poorer gentry.

" An interesting illustration of this [and of the class-feeling in education at this time] is supplied," says Mr Whiston, " by the narrative of what took place—

" when the Cathedral Church of Canterbury was altered from monks to secular men of the clergy, viz. : prebendaries or canons, petty-canons, choristers and scholars. At this erection were present, Thomas Cranmer, archbishop, with divers other commissioners. And nominating and electing such convenient and fit persons as should serve for the furniture of the said Cathedral church according to the new foundation, it came to pass that, when they should elect the children of the Grammar school, there were of the commissioners more than one or two who would have none admitted but sons or younger brethren of gentlemen. As for other, husbandmen's children, they were more meet, they said, for the plough, and to be artificers, than to occupy the place of the learned sort ; so that they wished none else to be put to school, but only gentlemen's children. Whereunto the most reverend father, the Archbishop, being of a contrary mind, said, ' That he thought it not indifferent so to order the matter ; for,' said he, ' poor men's children are many times endued with more singular gifts of nature, which are also the gifts of God, as, with eloquence, memory, apt pronunciation, sobriety, and such like ; and also commonly more apt to apply their study, than is the gentleman's son, delicately educated.' Hereunto it was on the other part replied, ' that it was meet for the ploughman's son to go to plough, and the artificer's son to apply the trade of his parent's vocation ; and the gentleman's children are meet to have the knowledge of government and rule in the commonwealth. For we have,' said they, ' as much need of ploughmen as any other state ; and all sorts of men may not go to school.' ' I grant,' replied the Archbishop, 'much of your meaning herein as needful in a commonwealth ; but yet utterly to exclude the ploughman's son and the poor man's son from the benefits of learning, as though they were unworthy to have

the gifts of the Holy Ghost bestowed upon them as well as upon
others, is as much to say, as that Almighty God should not be at
liberty to bestow his great gifts of grace upon any person, nor no-
where else but as we and other men shall appoint them to be em-
ployed, according to our fancy, and not according to his most goodly
will and pleasure, who giveth his gifts both of learning, and other
perfections in all sciences, unto all kinds and states of people in-
differently. Even so doth he many times withdraw from them and
their posterity again those beneficial gifts, if they be not thankful. If
we should shut up into a strait corner the bountiful grace of the Holy
Ghost, and thereupon attempt to build our fancies, we should make
as perfect a work thereof as those that took upon them to build the
Tower of Babel; for God would so provide that the offspring of our
first-born children should peradventure become most unapt to learn,
and very dolts, as I myself have seen no small number of them very
dull and without all manner of capacity. And to say the truth, I
take it, that none of us all here, being gentlemen born (as I think),
but had our beginning that way from a low and base parentage; and
through the benefit of learning, and other civil knowledge, for the
most part all gentlemen ascend to their estate.' Then it was again
answered, that the most part of the nobility came up by feats of arms
and martial acts. 'As though,' said the Archbishop, 'that the noble
captain was always unfurnished of good learning and knowledge to
persuade and dissuade his army rhetorically; who rather that way is
brought unto authority than else his manly looks. To conclude; the
poor man's son by pains-taking will for the most part be learned
when the gentleman's son will not take the pains to get it. And we
are taught by the Scriptures that Almighty God raiseth up from the
dunghill, and setteth him in high authority. And whensoever it
pleaseth him, of his divine providence, he deposeth princes unto a
right humble and poor estate. Wherefore, if the gentleman's son be
apt to learning, let him be admitted; if not apt, let the poor man's
child that is apt enter his room.' With words to the like effect."

R. WHISTON, *Cathedral Trusts*, p. 12—14.

The scandalous way in which the choristers and poor boys were
done out of their proportion of the endowments by the Cathedral
clergy, is to be seen in Mr Whiston's little book.

6. *Endowed Grammar Schools.* These were mainly founded for
citizens' and townsmen's children. Winchester (founded 1373) was
probably the only one that did anything before 1450 for the education of our gentry. Eton was not founded till 1440. The following
list of endowed schools founded before 1545, compiled for me by

Mr Brock from Carlisle's *Concise Description*, shows the dates of all known to him.

BEFORE 1450 A.D.

bef. 1162 Derby. Free School.
1195 St Alban's. Free Grammar School.
1198 St Edmund's, Bury. Fr. Sch.
1328 Thetford. Gr. Sch.
? 1327 Northallerton. Gr. Sch.
1332 Exeter. Gr. Sch.
1343 Exeter. High School.
bef. 1347 Melton Mowbray. Schools.
1373 Winchester College.
1384 Hereford. Gr. Sch.
1385 Wotton-under-Edge. Fr. Gr. Sch.
1395 or 1340 Penrith. Fr. Gr. Sch.
1399-1413 (Hen. IV.) Oswestry. Fr. Gr. Sch.
1418 Sevenoaks. Fr. Gr. Sch.
1422 Higham Ferrers. Fr. Gr. Sch.
1422-61 (Hen. VI.) Ewelme. Gr. Sch.
1440 Eton College.
1447 London. Mercers' School, but founded earlier.

SCHOOLS FOUNDED 1450—1545 A.D.

1461-83 (Edw. IV.) Chichester. The Prebendal School.
bef. 1477 Ipswich.[1] Gr. Sch.
1484 Wainfleet. Fr. Gr. Sch.
1485-1509 (Hen. VII.) or before. Kibroorth, near Market Harborough. Fr. Gr. Sch.
bef. 1486 Reading. Gr. Sch.
1486 Kingston upon Hull. Fr. Gr. Sch.

1487 Stockport. Gr. Sch.
1487 Chipping Campden. Fr. Gr. Sch.
1491 Sudbury. Fr. Gr. Sch.
bef. 1495 Lancaster. Fr. Gr. Sch.
1497 Wimborne Minster. Fr. Gr. Sch.
time of Hen. VII., 1485-1509 King's Lynn. Gr. Sch.
1502-52 Macclesfield. Fr. Gr. Sch.
1503 Bridgenorth. Fr. Sch.
1506 Brough *or* Burgh *under* Stainmore. Fr. Sch.
1507 Enfield. Gr. Sch.
1507 Farnworth, in Widnes, near Prescot. Fr. Gr. Sch.
ab. 1508 Cirencester. Fr. Gr. Sch.
1509 Guildford. Royal Gr. Sch.
t. Hen. VIII. 1509-47 Peterborough. Gr. Sch.
t. Hen. VIII. 1509-47 Basingstoke. Gr Sch.
t. Hen. VIII. 1509-47 Plymouth. Gr. Sch.
t. Hen. VIII. 1509-47 Warwick. College or Gr. Sch.
t. Hen. VIII. 1509-47 Earl's Colne, near Halsted. Fr. Gr. Sch.
t. Hen. VIII. 1509-47 Carlisle. Gr. Sch.
1512 Southover and Lewes. Fr. Gr. Sch.
1513 Nottingham. Fr. Sch.
1515 Wolverhampton. Fr. Gr. Sch.
1517 Aylesham. Fr. Gr. Sch.
1512-18 London.[2] St Paul's Sch.

---

[1] Farewell, in Oxford my college cardynall !
Farewell, in *Ipsewich, my schole gramaticall !*
Yet oons farewell ! I say, I shall you never see !
Your somptious byldyng, what now avaylletho me ?
Metrical Visions [Wolsey.] by George Cavendish, in his Life of Wolsey, (ed. Singer, ii. 17). Wolsey's Letter of Directions about his school should be consulted. It is printed.

[2] Colet's Statutes for St Paul's School are given in Howard Staunton's *Great Schools of England*, p. 179-85.

1520 Bruton or Brewton. Fr. Gr. Sch.
ab. 1520 Rolleston, nr. Burton-upon-Trent. Fr. Gr. Sch.
bef. 1521 Tenterden. Fr. Sch.
1521 Milton Abbas, near Blandford. Fr. Gr. Sch.
1522 Taunton. Fr. Gr. Sch.
1522 Biddenden, near Cranbrook. Free Latin Gr. Sch.
bef. 1524-5 Manchester. Fr. Gr. Sch.
1524 Berkhampstead. Fr. Gr. Sch.
1526 Pocklington. Fr. Gr. Sch.
1526 Childrey, near Wantage. Fr. Sch.
bef. 1528 Cuckfield. Fr. Gr. Sch.
1528 Gloucester. Saint Mary de Crypt. Fr. Gr. Sch.
1528 Grantham. Fr. Gr. Sch.
1530 Stamford, or Stanford. Fr. Gr. Sch.
1530 Newark-upon-Trent. Fr. Gr. Sch.
bef. Reform. Norwich. Old Gr. Sch.
t. Ref. Loughborough. Fr. Gr. Sch.

1532 Horsham. Fr. Sch.
1533 Bristol. City Fr. Gr. Sch.
ab. 1533 Newcastle-upon-Tyne. Royal Gr. Sch.
ab. 1535 Stoke, near Clare. Fr. Gr. Sch.
1541 Brecknock. Gr. Sch.
1541 Ely. Fr. Sch.
1541 Durham. Gr. Sch.
1541-2 Worcester. The King's [t. i. Cathedral Grammar] or College School.
1542 Canterbury. The King's School.
1542 Rochester. The King's Sch.[1]
1542 Findon, properly Thingdon, near Wellingborough. Fr. Sch.
1542 Northampton. Fr. Gr. Sch.
1543 Abergavenny. Fr. Gr. Sch.
1544 Chester. [Cathedral] Gr., or King's School.
1544 Sutton Coldfield. Gr. Sch.
bef. 1545 Gloucester. Cathedral [t. i. King's], or College School.
1545 St Mary of Ottery. Gr. Sch.
bef. 1547 Wisbech. Gr. Sch.
bef. 1549 Wellington. Gr. Sch.

About 1174 A.D., Fitzstephen speaks of the London schools and scholars thus:—I use Pegge's translation, 1772, to which Mr Chappell referred me,—

"The three principal churches in London[2] are privileged by grant and ancient usage with schools, and they are all very flourishing. Often indeed through the favour and countenance of persons eminent in philosophy, more schools are permitted. On festivals, at those churches where the Feast of the Patron Saint is solemnized, the masters convene their scholars. The youth, on that occasion, dispute, some in the demonstrative way, and some logically. These produce their enthymemes, and those the more perfect syllogisms. Some, the better to shew their parts, are exercised in disputation, contending with one another, whilst others are put upon establishing some truth by way of illustration. Some sophists endeavour to apply, on feigned topics, a vast heap and flow of words, others to impose upon you with

[1] 'That there was a school at Rochester before Henry VIII.'s time is proved by our Statutes, which speak of the *Schola Grammaticalis* as being *ruinosa & admodum deformis.*' R. Whiston.
[2] Pegge concludes these to have been St Paul's, Bow, and Martin's le Grand.

false conclusions. As to the orators, some with their rhetorical harangues employ all the powers of persuasion, taking care to observe the precepts of art, and to omit nothing opposite to the subject. The boys of different schools wrangle with one another in verse ; contending about the principles of Grammar, or the rules of the Perfect Tenses and Supines. Others there are, who in Epigrams, or other compositions in numbers, use all that low ribaldry we read of in the Ancients ; attacking their school-masters, but without mentioning names, with the old Fescennine licentiousness, and discharging their scoffs and sarcasms against them ; touching the foibles of their schoolfellows, or perhaps of greater personages, with true Socratic wit, or biting them more keenly with a Theonine tooth : The audience, fully disposed to laugh,

> ' With curling nose ingeminate the peals.' "

Of the sports of the boys, Fitzstephen gives a long description. On Shrove-Tuesday, each boy brought his fighting cock to his master, and they had a cock-fight all morning in the school-room.[1] After dinner, football in the fields of the suburbs, probably Smithfield. Every Sunday in Lent they had a sham-fight, some on horseback, some on foot, the King and his Court often looking on. At Easter they played at the Water-Quintain, charging a target, which if they missed, souse they went into the water. ' On holidays in summer the pastime of the youths is to exercise themselves in archery, in running, leaping, wrestling, casting of stones, and flinging to certain distances, and lastly with bucklers.' At moonrise the maidens danced. In the winter holidays, the boys saw boar-fights, hog-fights, bull and bear-baiting, and when ice came they slid, and skated on the legbones of some animal, punting themselves along with an iron-shod pole, and charging one another. A set of merry scenes indeed.

" In general, we are assured by the most learned man of the thirteenth century, Roger Bacon, that there never had been so great an appearance of learning, and so general an application to study, in so many different faculties, as in his time, when schools were erected in every city, town, burgh, and castle." (Henry's Hist. of England, vol. iv. p. 472-3.)

In the twenty-fifth year of Henry VI., 1447, four Grammar Schools were appointed to be opened in London[2] for the education of

---

[1] The custom of boys bringing cocks to masters has left a trace at Sedburgh, where the boys pay a sum every year on a particular day (Shrove-Tuesday ?) as "cock-penny." Quick.

[2] On the London Schools, see also Sir George Buc's short *cap*. 36, " Moore of

the City youth (*Carlisle*). But from the above lists it will be seen that Grammar Schools had not much to do with the education of our nobility and gentry before 1450 A.D.

Of Eton studies, the Paston Letters notice only Latin versifying, but they show us a young man supposed to be nineteen, still at school, having a smart pair of breeches for holy days, falling in love, eating figs and raisins, proposing to come up to London for a day or two's holiday or lark to his elder brother's, and having 8*d.* sent him in a letter to buy a pair of slippers with. William Paston, a younger brother of John's, when about nineteen years old, and studying at Eton, writes on Nov. 7, 1478, to thank his brother for a noble in gold, and says,

"my creanser (creditor) Master Thomas (Stevenson) heartily recommendeth him to you, and he prayeth you to send him some money for my commons, for he saith ye be twenty shillings in his debt, for a month was to pay for when he had money last ; also I beseech you to send me a hose cloth, one for the holy days of some colour, and another for working days (how coarse soever it be, it maketh no matter), and a stomacher and two shirts, and a pair of slippers : and if it like you that I may come with Alweder by water "—would they take a pair-oar and pull down ? (the figs and raisins came up by a barge ;)—" and sport me with you at London a day or two this term-time, then ye may let all this be till the time that I come, and then I will tell you when I shall be ready to come from Eton by the grace of God, who have you in his keeping." *Paston Letters*, modernised, vol. 2, p. 129.

This is the first letter ; the second one about the figs, raisins, and love-making (dated 23 Feb. 1478-9) is given at vol. ii. p. 122-3.

Tusser, who was seized as a Singing boy for the King's Chapel, lets us know that he got well birched at Eton.

> " From Paul's I went · to Eton sent
> To learn straightways · the Latin phrase
> When fifty-three · stripes given to me
> At once I had :

other Schooles in London," in his *Third Vniuersitie of England* (t. i. London). He notices the old schools of the monasteries, &c., 'in whose stead there be some few founded lately by good men ' as the Merchant Taylors, and Thomas Sutton, founder of the great new Hospitall in the Charter house, [who] hath translated the Tenis court to a Grammar Schoole . . for 30 schollers, poore mens children . . There be also other Triuiall Schooles for the bringing up of youth in good literature, *viz.*, in S. *Magnus*, in S. *Michaels*, in S. *Thomas*, and others.

For fault but small · or none at all
It come to pass · thus beat I was.
See, Udall,[1] see · the mercy.of thee
To me poor lad !"

I was rather surprised to find no mention of any Eton men in the first vol. of Wood's *Athenæ Oxonienses* (ed. Bliss) except two, who had first taken degrees at Cambridge, Robert Aldrich and William Alley, the latter admitted at Cambridge 1528 (Wood, p. 375, col. 2). Plenty of London men are named in Wood, vol. 1. No doubt in early times the Eton men went to their own foundation, King's (or other Colleges at) Cambridge, while the Winchester men went to their foundation, New College, or elsewhere at Oxford. In the first volume of Bliss's edition of Wood, the following Winchester men are noticed :

p. 30, col. 2, William Grocyn, educated in grammaticals in Wykeham's school near Winchester.

p. 78, col. 2, William Horman, made fellow of New Coll. in 1477. Author of the *Vulgaria Puerorum*, &c. (See also Andrew Borde, p. xxxiv, above, note.)

p. 379, col. 2, John Boxall, Fellow of New Coll. 1542.

402, col. 2, Thomas Hardyng ,, ,, ,, 1536.

450, col. 2, Henry Cole ,, ,, ,, 1523.

469, col. 1, Nicholas Saunders ,, ,, ,, 1548.

678, col. 2, Richard Haydock ,, ,, ,, 1590.

That the post-Reformation Grammar Schools did not at first educate as many boys as the old monastic schools is well known. Strype says,

" On the 15th of January, 1562, Thomas Williams, of the Inner Temple, esq. being chosen speaker to the lower house, was presented to the queen : and in his speech to her . . took notice of the want of schools ; that at least an hundred were wanting in England which before this time had been, [being destroyed (I suppose he meant) by the dissolution of monasteries and religious houses, fraternities and colleges.] He would have had England continually flourishing with ten thousand scholars, which the schools in this nation formerly brought up. That from the want of these good schoolmasters sprang up ignorance : and covetousness got the livings by impropriations ; which was a decay, he said, of learning, and by it the tree of know-

---

[1] Udall became Master of Eton about 1534.

ledge grew downward, not upward; which grew greatly to the dishonour, both of God and the commonwealth. He mentioned likewise
the decay of the universities; and how that great market-towns were
without schools or preachers: and that the poor vicar had but 20*l.*
[or some such poor allowance,] and the rest, being no small sum, was
impropriated. And so thereby, no preacher there; but the people,
being trained up and led in blindness for want of instruction, became
obstinate: and therefore advised that this should be seen to, and impropriations redressed, notwithstanding the laws already made [which
favoured them].—Strype, *Annals of the Reformation,* vol. i. p. 437.

Of the Grammar Schools in his time (A.D. 1577) Harrison says:

Besides these universities, also there are a great number of
Grammer Schooles throughout the realme, and those verie liberallie
endued for the better relief of pore scholers, so that there are not
manie corporate townes, now under the queene's dominion that have
not one Gramer Schole at the least, with a sufficient living for a
master and usher appointed to the same.

There are in like manner divers collegiat churches, as Windsor,
Wincester, Eaton, Westminster (in which I was sometime an unpro-
fitable Grammarian under the reverend father, master Nowell, now
dean of Paules) and in those a great number of pore scholers, dailie
maintained by the liberality of the founders, with meat, bookes, and
apparell; from whence after they have been well entered in the
knowledge of the Latine and Greek tongs, and rules of versifying
(the triall whereof is made by certain apposers, yearlie appointed to
examine them), they are sent to certain especiall houses in each
universitie[1], where they are received & trained up in the points of
higher knowledge in their privat halls till they be adjudged meet to
show their faces in the schooles, as I have said alreadie.

Greek was first taught at a public school in England by Lillye
soon after the year 1500. This was at St Paul's School in London,
then newly established by Dean Colet, and to which Erasmus alluded
as the best of its time in 1514, when he said that he had in three
years taught a youth more Latin than he could have acquired in any
school in England, *ne Liliana quidem excepta,* not even Lillye's
excepted. (Warton, iii. 1.) The first schoolmaster who stood up for
the study of English was, I believe, Richard Mulcaster, of King's
College, Cambridge, and Christ Church, Oxford. In 1561 he was
appointed the first head-master of Merchant-Taylors School in
London, then just founded as a feeder or pro-seminary for St John's

---

[1] The perversion of these elections by bribery is noticed by Harrison in the
former extract from him on the Universities.

College, Oxford (*Warton*, iii. 282). In his Elementarie, 1582, he has a long passage on the study of English, the whole of which I print here, at Mr Quick's desire, as it has slipt out of people's minds, and Mulcaster deserves honour for it :—

"But bycause I take vpon me in this Elementarie, besides som frindship to secretaries for the pen, and to correctors for the print, to direct such peple as teach childern to read and write English, and the *reading* must nedes be such as the writing leads vnto, thererfor, (*sic*) befor I medle with anie particular precept, to direct the Reader, I will thoroughlie rip vp the hole certaintie of our English writing, so far furth and with such assurance, as probabilitie can make me, bycause it is a thing both proper to my argument, and profitable to my cuntrie. For our naturall tung being as beneficiall vnto vs for our nedefull deliuerie, as anie other is to the peple which vse it : & hauing as pretie, and as fair obseruations in it, as anie other hath : and being as readie to yield to anie rule of Art, as anie other is : why should I not take som pains to find out the right writing of ours, as other cuntrimen haue don to find the like in theirs ? & so much the rather, bycause it is pretended, that the writing thereof is meruellous vncertain, and scant to be recouered from extreme confusion, without som change of as great extremitie ? I mean therefor so to deall in it, as I maie wipe awaie that opinion of either vncertaintie for confusion, or impossibilitie for direction, that both the naturall English maie haue wherein to rest, & the desirous st[r]anger maie haue whereby to learn. For the performance whereof, and mine own better direction, I will first examin those means, whereby other tungs of most sacred antiquitie haue bene brought to Art and form of discipline for their right writing, to the end that by following their waie, I maie hit vpon their right, and at the least by their president deuise the like to theirs, where the vse of our tung, & the propertie of our dialect will not yeild flat to theirs. That don, I will set all the varietie of our now writing, & the vncertaine force of all our letters, in as much certaintie, as anie writing can be, by these seuen precepts,—1. *Generall rule*, which concerneth the propertie and vse of ech letter : 2. *Proportion* which reduceth all words of one sound to the same writing : 3. *Composition*, which teacheth how to write one word made of mo : 4. *Deriuation*, which examineth the ofspring of euerie originall : 5. *Distinction* which bewraieth the difference of sound and force in letters by som writen figure or accent : 6. *Enfranchisment*, which directeth the right writing of all incorporat foren words : 7. *Prerogatiue*, which declareth a reseruation, wherein common vse will continew hir precedence in our En[g]lish writing, as she hath don euerie where else, both for the form of the letter, in som places, which likes the pen better : and for the difference in writing, where som particular caueat will chek a common rule. In all these seuen I will so examin the particularities of our tung, as either nothing shall

seme strange at all, or if anie thing do seme, yet it shall not
seme so strange, but that either the self same, or the verie like vnto
it, or the more strange then it is, shal appear to be in, those things,
which ar more familiar vnto vs for extraordinarie learning, then
required of vs for our ordinarie vse. And forasmuch as the eie will
help manie to write right by a sene president, which either cannot
vnderstand, or cannot entend to vnderstand the reason of a rule,
therefor in the end of this treatis for right writing, I purpos to set
down a generall table of most English words, by waie of president, to
help such plane peple, as cannot entend the vnderstanding of a rule,
which requireth both time and conceit in perceiuing, but can easilie
run to a generall table, which is readier to their hand. By the which
table I shall also confirm the right of my rules, that theie hold
thoroughout, & by multitude of examples help som maim (so) in
precepts. Thus much for the right writing of our English tung, which
maie seme (so) for a preface to the principle of *Reading*, as the matter
of the one is the maker of the other.—1582. Rich^d. Mulcaster. The
First Part of the Elementarie, pp. 53-4.

Brinsley follows Mulcaster in exhorting to the study of English :

"there seemes vnto mee, to bee a verie maine want in all our
Grammar schooles generally, or in the most of them ; whereof I haue
heard som great learned men to complain ; That there is no care had
in respect, to traine vp schollars so as they may be able to expresse
their minds purely and readily in our owne tongue, and to increase
in the practice of it, as well as in the Latine or Greeke ; whereas our
chiefe indeuour should bee for it, and that for these reasons. 1.
Because that language which all sorts and conditions of men amongst
vs are to haue most vse of, both in speech & writing, is our
owne natiue tongue. 2. The purity and elegancie of our owne
language is to be esteemed a chiefe part of the honour of our
nation : which we all ought to aduance as much as in vs lieth. As
when Greece and Rome and other nations haue most florished, their
languages also haue beene most pure : and from those times of Greece
& Rome, wee fetch our chiefest patterns, for the learning of their
tongues. 3. Because of those which are for a time trained vp in
schooles, there are very fewe which proceede in learning, in compari-
son of them that follow other callings.

John Brinsley, *The Grammar Schoole*, p. 21, 22.
His " Meanes to obtaine this benefit of increasing in our English
tong, as in the Latin," are
1. Daily vse of Lillies rules construed.
2. Continuall practice of English Grammaticall translations.
3. Translating and writing English, with some other Schoole
exercises.   *Ibid.*, side-notes, p. 22, 23.

On this question of English boys studying English, let it be
remembered that in this year of grace 1867, in all England there is

just one public school at which English is studied historically—the City of London School—and that in this school it was begun only last year by the new Head-Master, the Rev. Edwin A. Abbot, all honour to him. In every class an English textbook is read, *Piers Plowman* being that for the highest class. This neglect of English as a subject of study is due no doubt to tutors' and parents' ignorance. None of them know the language historically; the former can't teach it, the latter don't care about it; why should their boys learn it? Oh tutors and parents, there are such things as asses in the world.

Of the school-life of a Grammar-school boy in 1612 we may get a notion from Brinsley's p. 296, "chap. xxx. Of Schoole times, intermissions and recreations," which is full of interest. '1. The Schoole-time should beginne at sixe: all who write Latine to make their exercises which were giuen ouernight, in that houre before seuen'. —To make boys punctual, 'so many of them as are there at sixe, to haue their places as they had them by election[1] or the day before: all who come after six, euery one to sit as he commeth, and so to continue that day, and vntill he recouer his place againe by the election of the fourme or otherwise. . . If any cannot be brought by this, them to be noted in the blacke Bill by a speciall marke, and feele the punishment thereof: and sometimes present correction to be vsed for terrour. . . Thus they are to continue vntill nine [at work in class], signified by Monitours, Subdoctour or otherwise. Then at nine . . to let them to haue a quarter of an houre at least, or more, for intermission, eyther for breakefast . . or else for the necessitie of euery one, or their honest recreation, or to prepare their exercises against the Masters comming in. [2.] After, each of them to be in his place in an instant, vpon the knocking of the dore or some other sign . . so to continue vntill eleuen of the clocke, or somwhat after, to counteruaile the time of the intermission at nine.

(3.) To be againe all ready, and in their places at one, in an instant; to continue vntill three, or halfe an houre after: then to haue another quarter of an houre or more, as at nine for drinking and necessities; so to continue till halfe an houre after fiue : thereby in

---

[1] See p. 273-4, 'all of a fourme to name who is the best of their fourme, and who is the best next him '.

that halfe houre to counteruaile the time at three ; then to end so as
was shewed, with reading a peece of a Chapter, and with singing two
staues of a Psalme : lastly with prayer to be vsed by the Master.'

To the objectors to these intermissions at nine and three, who may
reproach the schoole, thinking that they do nothing but play,
Brinsley answers,—' 2. By this meanes also the Schollars may bee
kept euer in their places, and hard to their labours, without that
running out to the Campo (as the[y] tearme it) at school times, and
the manifolde disorders thereof ; as watching and striuing for the
clubbe,[1] and loytering then in the fields ; some hindred that they
cannot go forth at all. (5.) it is very requisite also, that they should
have weekly one part of an afternoone for recreation, as a reward of
their diligence, obedience and profiting ; and that to be appointed at
the Masters discretion, eyther the Thursday, after the vsuall custom ;
or according to the best opportunity of the place. . . All recreations
and sports of schollars, would be meet for Gentlemen. Clownish
sports, or perilous, or yet playing for money, are no way to be
admitted.'

On the age at which boys went to school, Brinsley says, p. 9,

" For the time of their entrance with vs, in our countrey schooles,
it is commonly about 7. or 8. yeares olde : six is very soone. If any
begin so early, they are rather sent to the schoole to keepe them from
troubling the house at home, and from danger, and shrewd turnes,
then for any great hope and desire their friends haue that they should
learne anything in effect."

To return from this digression on Education. Enough has been
said to show that the progress of Education, in our sense of the
word, was rather from below upwards, than from above downwards ;
and I conclude that the young people to whom the *Babees Boke*, &c.,
were addressed, were the children of our nobility, knights, and squires,
and that the state of their manners, as left by their home training,
was such as to need the inculcation on them of the precepts contained
in the Poems. If so, dirty, ill-mannered, awkward young gawks,
must most of these hopes of England have been, to modern notions.
The directions for personal cleanliness must have been much needed
when one considers the small stock of linen and clothes that men not

---

[1] ? key of the Campo, see pp. 299 and 300, or a club, the holder of which had a
right to go out.

rich must have had ; and if we may judge from a passage in Edward
the Fourth's *Liber Niger*, even the King himself did not use his
footpan every Saturday night, and would not have been the worse for
an occasional tubbing :—

"This barbour shall have, every satyrday at nyght, *if* it please
the Kinge to cleanse his head, legges, or feet, and for his shaving,
two loves, one picher wyne. And the ussher of chambre ought to
testyfye if this is necessaryly dispended or not."

So far as appears from Edward the Fourth's *Liber Niger Domus*, soap
was used only for washing clothes. The yeoman lavender, or washer
man, was to take from the Great Spicery ' as muche whyte soape,
greye, and blacke, as can be thought resonable by preufe of the
Countrollers,' and therewith 'tenderly to waysshe . . the stuffe for
the Kinges propyr persone' (*II. Ord.* p. 85) ; but whether that
cleansing material ever touched His Majesty's sacred person (except
doubtless when and if the barber shaved him), does not appear. The
Ordinances are considerate as to sex, and provide for "weomen
lavendryes" for a Queen, and further that "these officers oughte to
bee sworne to keepe the chambre counsaylle." But it is not for one
of a nation that has not yet taken generally to tubbing and baths,
or left off shaving, to reproach his forefathers with want of cleanliness, or adherence to customs that involve contradiction of the
teachings of physiologists, and the evident intent of Nature or the
Creator. Moreover, reflections on the good deeds done, and the high
thoughts thought, by men of old dirtier than some now, may prevent
us concluding that because other people now talk through their
noses, and have manners different from our own, they and their in-
stitutions must be wholly abominable ; that because others smell
when heated, they ought to be slaves ; or that eating peas with a
knife renders men unworthy of the franchise. The temptation to
value manners above morals, and pleasantness above honesty, is one
that all of us have to guard against. And when we have held to a
custom merely because it is old, have refused to consider fairly the
reasons for its change, and are inclined to grumble when the change
is carried out, we shall be none the worse for thinking of the people,
young and old, who, in the time of Harrison and Shakspere, the "For-

gotten Worthies "[1] and Raleigh, no doubt 'hated those nasty new oak houses and chimnies,' and sighed for the good old times :

" And yet see the change, for when our houses were builded of willow, then had we oken men ; but now that our houses are come to be made of oke, our men are not onlie become willow, but a great manie through Persian delicacie crept in among vs, altogither of straw, which is a sore alteration. . . Now haue we manie chimnies, and yet our tenderlings complaine of rheumes, catarhs and poses. Then had we none but reredosses, and our heads did neuer ake.[2] For as the smoke in those daies was supposed to be a sufficient harduing for the timber of the house ; so it was reputed a far better medicine to keepe the goodman and his familie from the quack or pose, wherewith as then verie few were oft acquainted." *Harrison*, i. 212, col. 1, quoted by Ellis.

If rich men and masters were dirty, poor men and servants must have been dirtier still. William Langlande's description of Hawkyn's one metaphorical dress in which he slept o' nightes as well as worked by day, beslobbered (or by-*moled*, bemauled) by children, was true of the real smock ; flesh-moths must have been plentiful, and the sketch of Coveitise, as regards many men, hardly an exaggeration :

. . as a bonde-man of his bacon · his berd was bi-draveled,
With his hood on his heed · a lousy hat above,
And in a tawny tabard · of twelf wynter age
Al so torn and baudy · and ful of lys crepyng,
But if that a lous[3] couthe · han lopen the bettre,

[1] See Mr Froude's noble article in *The Westminster Review*, No. 3, July, 1852 (lately republished by him in a collection of Essays, &c.).

[2] Their eyes must have smarted. The natives' houses in India have (generally) no chimneys still, and Mr Moreshwar says the smoke *does* make your eyes water.

[3] Mouffet is learned on the Louse.

" In the first beginning whilest man was in his innocency, and free from wickednesse, he was subject to no corruption and filth, but when he was seduced by the wickednesse of that great and cunning deceiver, and proudly affected to know as much as God knew, God humbled him with divers diseases, and divers sorts of Worms, with Lice, Hand-worms, Belly-worms, others call *Termites*, small Nits and Acares . . a Lowse . . is a beastly Creature, and known better in Innes and Armies then it is welcome. The profit it bringeth, *Achilles* sheweth, *Iliad* I. in these words : *I make no more of him then I doe of a Lowse ;* as we have an English Proverb of a poor man, *He is not worth a Lowse.* The Lice that trouble men are either tame or wilde ones, those the *English* call *Lice,* and these *Crab-lice ;* the North *English* call them *Pert-lice,* that is, a petulant Lowse comprehending both kindes ; it is a certain sign of misery, and is sometimes the inevitable scourge of

She sholde noght han walked on that welthe · so was it thred-bare.
(*Vision*, Passus V. vol. 1, l. 2859-70, ed. Wright.)

In the *Kinge and Miller*, Percy folio, p. 236, when the Miller
proposes that the stranger should sleep with their son, Richard the
son says to the King

> " Nay, first," quoth Richard, " good fellowe, tell me true,
> hast thou noe creepers in thy gay hose?
> art thou not troabled with the Scabbado ?"

The colour of washerwomen's legs was due partly to dirt, I
suppose. The princess or queen Clarionas, when escaping with the
laundress as her assistant, is obliged to have her white legs reduced
to the customary shade of grey :

> Right as she should stoupe a-doun,
> The quene was tukked wel on high ;
> The lauender perceiued wel therbigh
> Hir white legges, and seid " ma dame,
> Youre shin boones might doo vs blame;
> Abide," she seid, " so mot I thee,
> More slotered thei most be."
> Asshes with the water she menged,
> And her white legges al be-sprenged.
> ab. 1440 A.D., *Syr Generides*, p. 218, ll. 7060-8.

. If in Henry the Eighth's kitchen, scullions lay about naked, or
tattered and filthy, what would they do elsewhere? Here is the
King's Ordinance against them in 1526 :

God." Rowland's *Mouffet's Theater of Insects*, p. 1090, ed. 1658 (published in
Latin, 1634). By this date we had improved. Mouffet says, " These filthy creatures
.. are hated more than Dogs or Vipers by our daintiest Dames," *ib.* p. 1093 ; and
again, p. 1097, " Cardan, that was a fancier of subtilties, writes that the *Carthusians*
are never vexed with Wall-lice, and he gives the cause, because they eat no flesh. . .
He should rather have alledged their cleanliness, and the frequent washing of their
beds and blankets, to be the cause of it, which when the *French*, the *Dutch*, and
Italians do less regard, they more breed this plague. But the English that take
great care to be cleanly and decent, are seldom troubled with them." Also, on p. 1092,
he says, 'As for dressing the body : all *Ireland* is noted for this, that it swarms almost
with Lice. But that this proceeds from the beastliness of the people, and want of
cleanly women to wash them is manifest, because the English that are more careful
to dress themselves, changing and washing their shirts often, having inhabited so
long in *Ireland*, have escaped that plague... Remedies. The *Irish* and *Iseland*
people (who are frequently troubled with Lice, and such as will fly, as they say, in
Summer) anoint their shirts with Saffron, and to very good purpose, to drive away
the Lice, but after six moneths they wash their shirts again, putting fresh Saffron
into the Lye.' Rowland's Mouffet (1634), *Theater of Insects*, p. 1092, ed. 1658.

F

" And for the better avoydyng of corruption and all uncleannesse
out of the Kings house, which doth ingender, danger of infection,
and is very noisome and displeasant unto all the noblemen and
others repaireing unto the same ; it is ordeyned by the Kings High-
nesse, that the three master cookes of the kitchen shall have everie
of them by way of reward yearly twenty marks, to the intent they
shall prouide and sufficiently furnish the said kitchens of such
scolyons as shall not goe *naked or in garments of such vilenesse as
they now doe, and have been acustomed to doe, nor lie in the nights
and dayes in the kitchens or ground by the fireside ;* but that they
of the said money may be found with honest and whole course
garments, without such uncleannesse as may be the annoyance of
those by whom they shall passe ". . .

That our commonalty, at least, in Henry VIII.'s time did stink
(as is the nature of man to do) may be concluded from Wolsey's
custom, when going to Westminster Hall, of

"holding in his hand a very fair orange, whereof the meat or
substance within was taken out, and filled up again with the part of
a sponge, wherein was vinegar, and other confections against the
pestilent airs ; the which he most commonly smelt unto, passing
among the press, or else when he was pestered with many suitors."
(*Cavendish,* p. 43.)

On the dirt in English houses and streets we may take the
testimony of a witness who liked England, and lived in it, and who
was not likely to misrepresent its condition,—Erasmus.   In a letter
to Francis, the physician of Cardinal Wolsey, says Jortin,

" Erasmus ascribes the plague (from which England was hardly
ever free) and the sweating-sickness, partly to the incommodious
form and bad exposition of the houses, to the filthiness of the streets,
and to the sluttishness within doors. The floors, says he, are commonly
of clay, strewed with rushes, under which lies unmolested an ancient
collection of beer, grease (?), fragments, bones, spittle, excrements [t.
i. urine] of dogs and cats [t. i. men,] and every thing that is nasty,
&c." (*Life of Erasmus,* i. 69, ed. 1808, referred to in Ellis, i. 328,
note.)

The great scholar's own words are,

Tum sola fere sunt argilla, tum scirpis palustribus, qui subinde sic
renovantur, ut fundamentum maneat aliquoties annos viginti, sub
se fovens sputa, vomitus, mictum canum et hominum, projectam
cervisiam, et piscium reliquias, aliasque sordes non nominandas.
Hinc mutato cœlo vapor quidam exhalatur, mea sententia minime
salubris humano corpori.

After speaking also *De salsamentis* (rendered ' *salt meat,* beef, pork, &c.,' by Jortin, but which *Liber Cure Cocorum* authorises us in translating 'Sauces'[1]), *quibus vulgus mirum in modum delectatur*, he says the English would be more healthy if their windows were made so as to shut out noxious winds, and then continues,

"Conferret huc, si vulgo parcior victus persuaderi posset, ac salsamentorum moderatior usus. Tum si publica cura demandaretur Ædilibus, ut viæ mundiores essent a cœno, mictuque : Curarentur et ea quæ civitati vicina sint. *Jortin's Life of Erasmus,* ed. 1808, iii. 44 (Ep. 432, C. 1815), No. VIII. Erasmus Rot. Francisco. Cardinalis Eboracencis Medico, S.

If it be objected that I have in the foregoing extracts shown the dark side of the picture, and not the bright one, my answer is that the bright one—of the riches and luxury in England—must be familiar to all our members, students (as I assume) of our early books, that the Treatises in this Volume sufficiently show this bright side, and that to me, as foolometer of the Society, this dark side seemed to need showing. But as *The Chronicle* of May 11, 1867, in its review of Mr Fox Browne's *English Merchants,* seems to think otherwise, I quote its words, p. 155, col. 2.

"All the nations of the world, says Matthew of Westminster, were kept warm by the wool of England, made into cloth by the men of Flanders. And while we gave useful clothing to other countries, we received festive garments from them in return. For most of our information on these subjects we are indebted to Matthew Paris, who tells us that when Alexander III. of Scotland was married to Margaret, daughter of Henry III., one thousand English knights appeared at the wedding in *cointises* of silk, and the next day each knight donned a new robe of another kind. This grand entertainment was fatal to sixty oxen, and cost the then Archbishop of York no less a sum than 4000 marks. Macpherson remarks on this great display of silk as a proof of the wealth of England under the Norman kings, a point which has not been sufficiently elaborated. In 1242 the streets of London were covered or shaded with silk, for the reception of Richard, the King's brother, on his return from the Holy Land. Few English-

---

[1] Prof. Brewer says that Erasmus, rejecting the Mediæval Latin and adopting the Classical, no doubt used *salsamenta* in its classical sense of salt-meat, and referred to the great quantity of it used in England during the winter, when no fresh meat was eaten, but only that which had been killed at the annual autumn slaughtering, and then salted down. Stall-fattening not being practised, the autumn was the time for fat cattle. *Salsamentum,* however, is translated in White and Riddle's Dictionary, "A. Fish-pickle, brine ; B. Salted or pickled fish (so usually in plural)."

men are aware of the existence of such magnificence at that early period ; while every story-book of history gives us the reverse of the picture, telling us of straw-covered floors, scarcity of body linen, and the like. Long after this, in 1367, it is recorded, as a special instance of splendour of costume, that 1000 citizens of Genoa were clothed in silk; and this tale has been repeated from age to age, while the similar display, at an earlier date, in England, has passed unnoticed."

Turning at last to notice the several pieces in the present volume, I have only to say of number 1, *The Babees Boke*, that I have not had time to search for its Latin original, or other copies of the text. Its specialty is its attributing so high birth to the Bele Babees whom it addresses, and its appeal to Lady Facetia to help its writer. Of the short alphabetic poems that follow,—*The A B C of Aristotle*, Nos. 2 and 3,—copies occur elsewhere ; and that in Harl. MS. 1304, which has a different introduction, I hope to print in the companion volume to this, already alluded to. No. 4, *Vrbanitatis*, I was glad to find, because of the mention of *the booke of urbanitie* in Edward the Fourth's Liber Niger (p. ii. above), as we thus know what the Duke of Norfolk of "Flodden Field" was taught in his youth as to his demeanings, how mannerly he should eat and drink, and as to his communication and other forms of court. He was not to spit or snite before his Lord the King, or wipe his nose on the table-cloth. Nos. 5 and 6, *The Lytylle Chyldrenes Lytil Boke or Edyllys Be*[1] (a title made up from the text) and *The Young Children's Book*, are differing versions of one set of maxims, and are printed opposite one another for contrast sake. *The Lytil Boke* was printed from a later text, and with an interlinear French version, by Wynkyn de Worde in ' *Here begynneth a lytell treatyse for to lerne Englisshe and Frensshe.*' This will be printed by Mr Wheatley in his Collection of Early Treatises on Grammar for the Society, as the copy in the Grenville Library in the Brit. Mus. is the only one known. (By the way, what member will find some additional tracts for this volume ? There must be some lying about somewhere.)

---

[1] What this *Edyllys Be* means, I have no idea, and five or six other men I have asked are in the same condition. A.S. *æþel* is noble, *æþeling*, a prince, a noble ; that may do for *edyllys*. *Be* may be for A B C, alphabet, elementary grammar of behaviour.

Other copies of this Lytil Boke are at Edinburgh, Cambridge, and Oxford. Of two of these Mr David Laing and Mr Henry Bradshaw have kindly given me collations, which are printed at the end of the Prefaces here. Of No. 7, *Stans Puer ad Mensam*, attributed to Lydgate —as nearly everything in the first half of the 15th century was—I have printed two copies, with collations from a third, the Jesus (Cambridge) MS. printed by Mr Halliwell in *Reliquiæ Antiquæ*, v. 1, p. 156-8, and reprinted by Mr W. C. Hazlitt in his *Early Popular Poetry*, ii. 23-8. Mr Hazlitt notices 3 other copies, in Harl. MS. 4011, fol. 1, &c. ; Lansdowne MS. 699 ; and Additional MS. 5467, which he collated for his text. There must be plenty more about the country, as in Ashmole MS. 61, fol. 16, back, in the Bodleian.[1] Of old printed editions Mr Hazlitt notes one "from the press of Caxton, but the only copy known is imperfect. It was printed two or three times by Wynkyn de Worde. Lowndes mentions two, 1518, 4to, and 1524, 4to ; and in the public library at Cambridge there is said by Hartshorne (*Book Rarities*, 156) to be a third without date. It is also appended to the various impressions of the *Boke of Nurture* by Hugh Rhodes." This is printed below, and its *Stans Puer* is Rhodes's own expansion of one of these shorter versions of the original Latin[2] (Part II. p. 30). No. 8 is an incomplete poem on Manners from the Lambeth MS. 853. Nos. 9 and 10 are short bits that Mr W. Aldis Wright was kind enough to send me. Of the latter of these Mr Thomas Wright says, "The verses at the bottom of p. 35, 'with this bytel,' &c., belong to a medieval story, which you will find, with the verses, in my 'Latin Stories' (printed for the Percy Society), pp. 28, 29. It is, in fact, the same story as King Lear and his Dauthers. You will find more about it in the note at the end of my volume, and another copy of the verses."

No. 11, *The Good Wijf*, is a mother's advice to her daughter as to her behaviour generally, her choice of a husband, and the management of her household. It bears trace of the greater freedom of action allowed to women in early times than now, a freedom shown

---

[1] P.S. Mr Hazlitt, iv. 366, notices two others in MS. Ashmole 59, art. 57, and in Cotton MS. Calig. A II. fol. 13, the latter of which and Ashmole 61, are, he says, of a different translation.

[2] See Hazlitt, iv. 366.

in Langlande's 'Cesse the souteresse' and 'Rose the dyssheres' in the celebrated alehouse scene (*Vision of Piers Pl.*), in Chaucer's Wif of Bathe, in women's membership of gilds, &c. The injunction not to get drunk *often*, as that would be shameful (l. 39), is a sign of the times. And the advice to the girl to scorn no wooer, whatsoever he might be (ll. 32-3), looks as if husbands were as scarce an article then as they are now. In 1838, Sir Frederic Madden printed a few copies of this poem for private distribution from a Henry the Sixth MS., which contained 35 stanzas against our 31, but the text is inferior to our Lambeth one, especially in the tags of the stanzas. This text Mr Hazlitt reprinted in the 1st volume of his most interesting collection of *Early Popular Poetry* (4 vols. J. R. Smith, £1), and I have not collated it with the text printed in the present collection, because Mr Hazlitt's volumes should be in all our members' hands. The Trinity College (Cambridge) MS. of the poem, Mr Aldis Wright has kindly collated with our text, in the notes to it. Another version of it, different in almost every stanza, is in the Porkington MS. No. 10, and this I hope to print for the Society some day or other. Mr Lumby will, I believe, print yet another version for us this year from the *Lancelot-of-the-Laik* MS.; and a MS. also containing the poem, Ashmole 61, fol. 7, has not been examined for or by me. Lastly, Mr Hazlitt notes that a poor copy of the text was printed in 1597 (in 33 stanzas) under the title of *The Northern Mothers Blessing. The Way of Thrift*[1]. *Written nine years before the death of G. Chaucer.* This latter date is possible, for I feel certain that all the copies above mentioned are but variations from some original type that has not yet turned up. The *Good Wiff* contains an odd instance of how even good editors are sometimes thrown off the scent. In it occurs the proverb, " aftir þe wrenne haþ veynes, Men must lete hir blood," that is, bleed her according to her tiny veins, or as we say, 'cut your coat according to your cloth,' spend according to your income.[2] On this Proverb in his Text, Mr Hazlitt says (*Early Popular Poetry*, vol. i. p. 187),

---

[1] This is a separate poem which I shall print. The vol. is 238 a. 13, in Brit. Mus.

[2] Cp. ' Ask your purse what you should buy'; ' Ken when to spend and when to spare, and ye needna be busy, and ye'll ne'er be bare,' from *Hislop*.

" The edition of 1597 reads :—

'After the wren has veines men may let blood.'

That is to say, at that season of the year when the young bird is of a certain growth, men shall, if they require it, undergo cupping ! In the MS., and in the edition of 1838 (Sir Frederic Madden's,) on the contrary, the line runs thus :—

'For aftir the wrenne hath veynes, men schalle late HIR blode.'

Sir Frederic Madden could make nothing of this passage [1], and in his Preface he expressly says that 'the researches made for this purpose [the illustration of it] have not proved successful.' It appears to me that the sense is figurative, and that what the author intended to convey was, that as soon as a person becomes full of substance, the world will fleece him or her, if he or she does not exercise vigilance. This construction is borne out completely by the context."

—("Which seems to indicate that the writer . . missed the point." *Hazlitt*, p. 183, n. 4. See too the *way-goose* note on 'away goes,' iv. 124.)

No. 12, *How the Wise Man tau3t his Sonne*, is the parallel of The Good Wife, is shorter than it, and written with less go and less detail. The advice about choosing a wife is extremely good, the way to treat her very judicious,—

      . .   softe & faire a man may tame
   Boþe herte and hynde, bucke & do,—

as is also the counsel not to be too hasty to fight and chide every one she complains of.[2] That ladies had a supply of pepper sauce on hand for servants (and husbands doubtless) as well as fresh salmon and lamprey (Part II. p. 45), we may gather from Wynkyn de Worde's warning to his Carver, "ladyes wyll soone be angry, for theyr thoughtes ben soone changed" (p. 279). In one point the Wise Man was a degenerate Englishman. The Toulmin Smith of his time would have rebuked him severely for advising his son (in lines 41-8, p. 49) to shirk his share of the work that in this self-governing land should have been his pride, because he must thereby displease his

---

[1] ? Sir Frederic says only, " One expression would seem to require illustration,— *Aftir the wrenne hathe veynes, men schalle late hir blode,*—but the researches made for this purpose have not proved successful. Could this phrase be found still in existence, it might perhaps afford reasonable grounds for localising the poem."

[2] The Cambridge MS. that Mr Hazlitt prints has a reason (not in our text) for the probable injustice of the wife's complaints,

   For women yn wrethe, they can not hyde,
   But sone they reyse a smokei rofe.—(p. 174, l. 120.)

neighbours or forswear himself, and get more ill-will than thanks. "England expects every man to do his duty" was not the Wise Man's sentiment. Ritson printed *The Wise Man* in his Pieces of Ancient Popular Poetry, 1791, p. 83-91, from the Harleian MS. 4596;[1] and Mr Hazlitt printed it in his Early Popular Poetry, vol. i. p. 169-77, from the Cambridge MS. Ff. ii. 38 (or MS. More 690). The Cambridge text is a later and longer one than the Lambeth copy in this volume, of which Mr Hazlitt did not know, and contains 188 lines to our 152, the chief expansions being about a man's duty to his wife; that he should not be jealous, as that'll make her worse; should treat her 'as reson ys,' and that he should not beat her. Resort to common women is also condemned ; and the arrangement of the stanzas is much altered. Mr Hazlitt gives no reason for his statement that "the success and reputation" of *The Wise Man* led, possibly at no great interval, to the production of "How the Goode Wif thaught hir Doughter." Imitations do not often beat originals, and *The Good Wife* is the better poem.[2] The text printed by Mr Hazlitt looks to me like an altered copy of the original poem, with a proverb in the first stanza imitated from *The Good Wife*. Still it is possible that the original of *The Wise Man* was the earlier poem, for in the *Luytel Caton* in the Vernon MS. (ab. 1375 A.D.), in Latin, French, and English,—about to be edited for us by Mr Brock,—occur these lines,

> Now hose wole, he may here
> In Englisch langage,
> *How þe wyse mon tauhte his sone*
> þat was of tendere age.

The Vernon version differs widely from the later ones printed by Mr Hazlitt and here, but, as their precursor, may have been earlier than the original of *The Good Wife*. The advice to the boy on his amusements is,

---

[1] 1596 he calls it. Mr Hazlitt corrects him.

[2] So in 1570-6 it is ladies first, *place aux dames*. '1570-1. Rd of Ryc. Jounes, for his lycense for pryntinge of a ballett of the comly behavyour for Ladyes and gentlewomen, iiijᵈ.' *Collier's Extracts from the Registers of the Stationers' Company*, ii. 15. 'xvijʰ die Julii, 1576. Ric Jones. Receyved of him, for his lycense to ymprinte a booke intituled how a younge gentleman may behave him self in all cumpanies, &c. viijᵈ·, and a copie.'

Take a Toppe, ȝif þou wolt pleye,
And not at þe hasardrye.
Vernon MS., fol. 310, col. 1, bottom.

Nos. 13 and 16 are just a page each of Recipes of dishes mentioned in this volume, to fill up blanks. No. 13 is an English *Dietorie*, and No. 14 its Latin original. ' Clear air and walking make good digestion' is a good maxim; ' to poor folk do thou no violence,' one needed, with its companion

To visite þe poore do þi diligence,
And on þe needi haue compassioun,
For good deedis causiþ mirþe in conscience,
And in heuene to haue greet possessioun.

A list of some of the other MSS. of the Poem is given at the foot of p. 58.

After the Recipes No. 16, come Hugh Rhodes's Boke of Nurture, and John Russell's Boke of Nurture with its accompanying illustrative notes and Treatises. Each of these Bokes has its separate Preface, as beforesaid, and to them I refer the reader ; only advising him to read Russell's text.

As to the Second Part of this volume, which contains a few French and Latin Poems on the same subjects of Manners and Meals as the English Poems of the First Part, and in illustration of them, I am not prepared to contend that French and Latin are Early English, but having broken the ice by printing the original Latin of two English Poems in the First Part opposite their translations, and being unable to give the Latin original of *Stans Puer* opposite the English versions of it, because there were two of them, I was obliged to put this Latin into an Appendix or Part II. There was another short poem in the same MS. that it would have been a shame to leave out ; and then came a most obliging and kind tempter in the person of Mr Thomas Wright, with a very interesting short volume of French Poems on Manners, edited by his late friend M. de Monmerqué, and with a reference to a Latin *Modus Cenandi* that might be the original of everything of the kind in French and English. What could one do but yield and be thankful ? However, punishment came for one's wandering from the paths of virtue and Early English, for that *Modus Cenandi* turned out to be no end of a plague ; in many places a corrupt text, written on very thin vellum, through which the ink of one side showed on the other, and both sides had faded. The consequence was, that after troubling Mr Brock and Mr T. Wright, and getting all that was gettable out of them, I was obliged to have recourse to the officers of the MS. Department in the Museum and worry them. Mr Scott kindly gave up much time to the difficult places, but some of them have beaten even him. Professor Seeley has been good enough to give me a literal English translation of the Latin pieces in Part II., but has often had to guess instead of translate. Monsieur Michelant, of the Imperial Library, courteously sent me the first French Poem in the same Part. Without the help of the gentlemen above named I could have made nothing of this Part II., and to them all I am greatly indebted. The ready way in which help is given to one, whenever it is asked for, is one of the pleasantest incidents of one's work.

It only remains for me to say that the woodcuts at the end of the book cost the Society nothing; that the freshness of my first interest in the poems which I once hoped to re-produce in these Forewords, has become dulled by circumstances and the length of time that the volume has been in the press—it having been set aside (by my desire) for the *Ayenbite*, &c.;—and that the intervention of other work has prevented my making the collection as complete as I had desired it to be. It is, however, the fullest verse one that has yet appeared on its subject, and will serve as the beginning of the Society's store of this kind of material.[1] If we can do all the English part of the work, and the Master of the Rolls will commission one of his Editors to do the Latin part, we shall then get a fairly complete picture of that Early English Home which, with all its shortcomings, should be dear to every Englishman now.

3, *St George's Square, N.W.*,
    5th June, 1867.

---

[1] If any member or reader can refer me to any other verse or prose pieces of like kind, unprinted, or that deserve reprinting, I shall be much obliged to him, and will try to put them in type.

www.ingramcontent.com/pod-product-compliance
Lightning Source LLC
Chambersburg PA
CBHW020329090426
42735CB00009B/1469